*Youth
library
work*

Youth library work

EXPLORATORY ESSAYS BY MELVYN P BARNES

CLIVE BINGLEY  LONDON

D153765

FIRST PUBLISHED 1968 BY CLIVE BINGLEY LTD
16 PEMBRIDGE ROAD LONDON W11
SET IN 10 ON 12 POINT LINOTYPE BASKERVILLE
AND PRINTED IN GREAT BRITAIN BY
THE CENTRAL PRESS (ABERDEEN) LTD
COPYRIGHT © MELVYN P BARNES 1968
ALL RIGHTS RESERVED
85157 054 2

Contents

Author's note

I should like to thank Miss L V Paulin MA FLA (County Librarian of Hertfordshire) for kindly allowing me to quote from the publication *Teenread* in chapter five; Mr S E Overal ALA (Borough Librarian of the London Borough of Waltham Forest) for supplying me with information concerning his youth library which I have used in chapter three; the staff of the Manchester Public Libraries interlending service and stack, for coping so patiently with my multitudinous requests for material; and Mrs Pauline Hull, who typed the manuscript so ably.

While engaged in the writing I shut myself away, deterred all intruders and became very disagreeable, so finally I wish to thank my wife for suffering my behaviour, and to her I dedicate this book.

MPB

Introduction

The starting point of this book is that comparatively modern phenomenon, the 'teenager'. Of course teenagers have always existed but it is only during the last twenty years or so that, as a group, they have made their existence aggressively evident to other sections of the community, and sometimes in most unpleasant ways. This has resulted in the term 'teenager' becoming now more widely used than 'adolescent', very often as a label with derogatory connotations.

Is today's adolescent any more rebellious or difficult than his predecessors? Some obviously are. But society has changed greatly in recent years—the rate of maturity has accelerated, the pace of living has increased, and in today's world there is very real uncertainty about the chances of living to a ripe old age. Insecurity is one of the perennial characteristics of adolescence, but environment can produce, in the extreme cases, a youthful philosophy of 'let's live today, and let tomorrow take care of itself'.

As adults, we realise the necessity of preparing for the future, and we realise too that in later adolescence the teenager will need to collect his attitudes into a responsible adult pattern. As librarians, we also know that the public library can help him in this, but it is here that we encounter our major problem. Many teenagers do not use public library services, particularly in the years immediately following the end of their school careers; various surveys have shown this, including most notably the *Crowther report* of 1959.

There are many reasons why this 'teenage drift' (as it has been called) takes place. Most of the reasons can be grouped together under one general statement: the teenager has comparatively little time on his hands, and he does not realise, of himself, how the public library can engage and supplement the many other activities which fill his life. The problem has existed, as have the apologia, for some time. There has been a considerable amount of writing about it in professional journals, and much discussion, but still we have not really got down to tackling the matter in practice. Some librarians blame the teenagers for lack of interest, and choose to believe that they will return to the library in later years; but their optimism is not necessarily justified and the claim is, at best, ' sour grapes '.

The problem remains. We must persuade teenagers to read books, although they have many other claims upon their time; we must encourage those who are already library members to continue to use our services; and we must attract those who have not previously been members to join the library. There is no single solution.

Should we, for example, provide a specialised service to this age group? If so, what type of service should it be? What are the advantages and disadvantages of establishing a separate intermediate department? These are some of the questions which librarians should be asking themselves, because the adolescent really does require more consideration from librarians than he has been generally receiving heretofore. He is, after all, on the brink of adulthood—though not yet an adult—and the successful transfer from the simplicity of the children's department to the breadth and complexity of the adult department requires a delicacy not often encountered in contemporary library services. To train boys and girls in the use of libraries while they are members of the children's department, and then just to drop them at the age of thirteen, can aggravate the problem we are trying to solve.

First, then, we need to know something about the teenagers themselves. Secondly, we need to understand the reasons for their apparent lack of interest in libraries. Thirdly, we need to decide how best to give a specialised service aimed directly at the thirteen to seventeen age group. Fourthly, stemming from this, we need to promote our services by co-operation with other agencies, and by using methods such as extension activities and booklists. These are the subjects of the five essays in this book.

This is not a comprehensive manual; there are already too many books which seek to tell librarians how to do things which they are mostly well qualified to decide for themselves. This is a collection of essays dealing with selected topics in youth library work, which are not intended to provide all the answers, but may, I hope, provoke readers to think afresh about an important subject

8

which has not been discussed in book form in Great Britain for
a number of years.

At the time of writing this book I am a member of the staff of
Manchester Public Libraries, and I must make it clear that the
views put forward in these essays are personal to me. In order to
sustain continuity, where I have quoted books or articles in the
text, full bibliographical details have not been given; they may be
obtained from the bibliography at the end of the book.

MPB

CHAPTER ONE:

The period of adolescence

In any activity directed at teenagers, a basic knowledge of adolescent psychology is vital. No apology is therefore made for opening this book with an essay on a subject which is at first sight unconnected with librarianship. As librarians, we need to be able to assist and understand teenagers among all sections of the community, and to make this assistance and understanding easier, we need to know more about the place of the teenager in society, the reasons for his likes and dislikes, and the established traits of the teenager as an individual.

The concise Oxford dictionary defines an adolescent as a ' person growing up, between childhood and manhood or womanhood '. For the casual enquirer this simple description may suffice; adolescence is, however, far more than just a period between two more or less rigidly defined ages.

First, it is important to differentiate between adolescence and puberty. Puberty is part of adolescence, and consists of purely physiological changes in the sexual and other organs which take place over a comparatively brief part of the adolescent period. Adolescence itself involves considerably more than the physical changes which occur at puberty; over eight years or so the adolescent develops in his attitudes, in his interests and capacities, and in his relations to others. If he does not develop physically and psychologically, he will enter adulthood under serious handicaps.

Although adolescence lasts approximately eight years in most cases, it is impossible to fix the period within precise age limits. Whereas physical growth is fairly well defined, with comparatively few accelerated or retarded cases, intellectual and social development can be uneven and extremely varied from one adolescent to another, and indeed this phase of development may begin as early as ten years of age and continue until the age of twenty one. On the average, however, adolescence is considered by most authorities to cover the years twelve to twenty in the case of girls, and fourteen to twenty in the case of boys. Girls normally enter adolescence with the arrival of puberty two years earlier than boys, but on reaching late adolescence physical and psychological development have reached a comparable stage in both sexes.

The characteristics of adolescence are not only brought about by the physical changes inherent in the period, although sexual growth is a factor to be taken into consideration. Society itself influences the adolescent in his thoughts and actions, by stipulating that a responsible social being should act in a certain manner. Authority, represented by the home, the school and other agencies, formulates the written and unwritten social code, and so influences the adolescent's behaviour. It may not, of course, influence him in the direction it intends, for a major characteristic of adolescence is the increasing conflict between his own wishes and those of authoritarian society; indeed the adolescent may take the other direction to such a degree that he reaches the stage generally known as ' delinquency '.

In addition to stipulating a code of conduct, the community is responsible for providing the adolescent's environment. The lives of many young people are far from settled; demolition of old houses, for example, or the necessity for a family to move from one part of the country to another in search of better employment prospects, may add to already confused minds. The adolescent has so many new things to think about, to come to terms with, that he needs a settled environment with a steady group of friends to enable him to find his place and develop the aptitudes required of a mature individual.

There are other general influences which exist today and did not exist, say, fifty years ago, and which introduce new factors to the subject of adolescent psychology. First, there is the influence of the mass media of communication, which gives rise to such present day controversy as that over the effects of television on teenage lawlessness; this is an aspect which will be briefly considered later in this essay. Secondly, there is the influence of ' the bomb '; the possibility of mass extermination of large sections of the human race is disregarded by many adults, who consider, more in hope than conviction, that it could never happen; yet to young people it is a possibility which affords no peace of mind and much apprehension for the future. When adults condemn teenagers for apparently wanting to enjoy themselves today and not thinking about tomorrow, they should realise that this factor ought to be taken into account and that young people are only reacting to a situation which is not of their own making.

Individual adolescents react in different ways to the influences of their physical changes and to the burdens and stimuli imposed upon them by the community. The minority of them which reacts violently has been responsible for labelling the period as one of stress and rebellion. Nevertheless, as adolescence is but one stage of physical and mental progress among several—and, moreover, a stage through which all human beings pass—it is possible to generalise and to list development characteristics common to most adolescents on their way to becoming adult citizens. These characteristics will be described under the following headings: emotional development; social development; intellectual development; heterosexual development; self identification; relations with home and authority; leisure.

EMOTIONAL DEVELOPMENT

The emotions are one component of the whole person. They are the safety valves of the intellect and the psyche and are essentially responses (in the form of anger, for example, or laughter) to physical or intellectual situations. They change and develop with age, however. Most people consider the adolescent to be highly ' emotional ', (ie dominated in his actions by emotional rather than intellectual criteria), but this is a generalisation; the most obvious manifestations are so conspicuous as to attract more attention. Thus we notice a teenager when he is behaving in an angry and loud manner.

How ' emotional ' is the average adolescent? The answer is, probably, that he is less outwardly emotional than his younger, non-adolescent, brother or sister, but his occasional outbursts of anger or self assertion are more effective than the outbursts of a young child, which adults tend to disregard. The adolescent has become more mature emotionally as he has grown older. As a child he was self centred, perhaps prone to tantrums and tears when frustrated; he was afraid of things he did not understand and tried continually to escape into worlds of his own; in fact, he behaved and thought in ways which we normally expect of children. During the period of adolescence his expressions of emotion must become more constructive, more rationally based, and he gradually learns to resolve problems as they arise, not to 'duck', or escape them, to face reality and to become less self centred. These are the necessary adjustments and controls which help to convert the child into the adult.

SOCIAL DEVELOPMENT

As a child progresses into adolescence, his need for acceptance by the adults with whom he comes into contact is complemented to a large extent by a need for acceptance by others of his own age. During adolescence this need becomes stronger and progressively more important to him, and the period becomes predominantly one of social development and social adjustment. He loses, if he is an average teenager, the self centredness he displayed in childhood and becomes essentially a member of a group.

Parents often find this upsetting, because the authority they previously were able to exert over their children may rapidly diminish as the home begins to take second place to the coffee bar, the discothèque, and the other places where the 'gangs' habitually gather. Many parents, however, soon come to realise that this emancipation from home is ultimately for the good, for the adolescent who does not mix with his contemporaries is likely to depend on his family for emotional support to a degree that could harm his later life. As a member of his group, the adolescent is not only developing responsibility and self identification; he is also taking the first steps in his heterosexual development and relations, leading ultimately to his finding a partner for life.

The group of agemates which the adolescent joins is sometimes called 'the gang' or 'the crowd', but is often referred to by psychologists as 'the adolescent peer group'. It is merely a way of describing the small gatherings of boys and girls, normally an equal number of each, that one observes in coffee bars, in the street, and in other places where teenagers gather. The members of the group probably live near one another, in many cases attend the same school or college, and have approximately the same home background.

Adults are often contemptuous or afraid of 'the group'. They see it as a threat, and prone to mischief and even violence; the word 'gang' has in fact become synonymous with rowdiness, theft and violence. Because crime—ranking second only to sex—has become an aspect of teenage activity which is prominently reported in the press, we tend to think of the adolescent peer group as a malignant organisation with no constructive developmental purpose. Nothing could be further from the truth. Except for the headline making minority—who do not concern us here —the adolescent obtains from his group certain advantages which lead to his social maturity and which cannot be adequately obtained from authority groups such as parents and teachers.

He begins to realise, for example, that when he does something for the group he is at the same time doing something for himself; thus he learns that his own self interest is incidental and should not be the mainspring of his actions. This enables him to develop an independent social consciousness, which is a facet of psychological maturity. Another function of the group is to offer security to the adolescent at a stage in his development when he is uncertain of himself; he is uncertain because he is passing through a period of rapid psychological and physical change, and can achieve some measure of security by mixing with others who have the same problems. In addition to giving him the support he needs, the group also gives him approval in matters regarding which teachers and parents often display only disapproval. His attitudes, the way he dresses and the type of music he likes are examples of things which are very real to him, and whereas they are often derided by adults they are approved by his peers.

On the whole, therefore, the group as a social unit has many advantages which outweigh its disadvantages, and the only serious disadvantage is its effect on the occasional solitary non-member. To its members it offers a feeling of security and practice in the art of sociability, among other things, and according to some psychologists is the most formative and influential single factor in the average adolescent's life.

INTELLECTUAL DEVELOPMENT

Various types of intelligence tests are in existence, and doubtless more will be devised, which when used by an expert can reveal the child's mental standard and thus provide a yardstick against which to chart his intellectual progress. No detail will be entered into here regarding these tests, for comprehensive works have already appeared on the subject, and some of them are listed in the bibliography. The only point to be made is that because intellectual development can be measured and charted it is therefore an aspect of child and adolescent psychology which is fairly clear cut, and about which certain facts are generally accepted.

During the adolescent period there is a phenomenal increase in mental capacity. Whereas children, even when very young, show a desire for facts and ask countless questions, an adolescent adds something to this—he wants explanations, not just facts. The child's brain is relatively undeveloped and his capacity for reasoning is limited, but in his late childhood and adolescence he no longer blindly accepts as truth the word of a parent or even of a teacher. He begins to think for himself, to question and demand evidence; in fact, to show signs of a healthily maturing mind. Teachers—and probably many librarians—already know this (sometimes to their embarrassment), and are aware of the need to justify anything they communicate to young people as fact.

Another way in which an adolescent's mental development can be clearly seen is in the way he approaches hobbies and interests. The child and the young adolescent will normally have many temporary interests, adopting new ones as frequently as they discard others. By the end of adolescence, however, the average young man or woman has settled down to a few regular interests which are pursued in great detail, and some of which may even be maintained for the rest of their lives. Reading is the obvious activity which concerns us here, and other mass media to a lesser extent. A librarian needs to know what young people read and— as far as this can be determined—what influences them in their choice.

HETEROSEXUAL DEVELOPMENT

An interest which in many cases overrides all others during the adolescent years is sex. In most cases an adolescent's physical development will take place quite gradually. Whereas his close friends were previously almost invariably members of his own sex, to the exclusion of members of the opposite sex, this gives way during adolescence to an increasing heterosexual attraction. This attraction is, of course, the normal result of a maturing body and mind, and after the first feelings of the novelty of the situation have been passed most adolescents will realise just how normal it is. But they are not always helped by their parents to see it as normal; some parents who feel that their adolescent children are too young to associate regularly with members of the opposite sex, and who inhibit them by showing their disapproval, may do their children considerable harm.

At some stage during their adolescence most boys and girls will pass through a period of intense attraction toward members of the opposite sex (and often first of all, though briefly, to their own). Adult censure of this is unwarranted, particularly as in most cases the acute period is transitory. It is also harmless, since it tends to involve contact with many members of the opposite sex rather than any single one regularly, and probably results far more rarely in actual sexual activity than the popular press would have us believe. In fact, far from being a period fraught with sexual dangers, this stage encompasses normal sexual development.

For all their brashness on the subject of heterosexual relationships, it is as well to realise that part of the reason for establishing such relationships lies in the need of young people for some kind of security among their agemates. When ' dating ' assumes greater sexual than social significance, this aspect of a teenager's life can cause him much anxiety and bewilderment, as well as feelings of guilt and occasionally fear. If he receives more admonishment than advice from his elders, a mature attitude toward sex will not be developed very easily. Young people are sometimes reluctant to seek help from their parents about sexual matters. Instruction is given in schools, although this is predominantly biological rather than practically helpful.

Have we as librarians a task to perform in sex education? We have, in that we must make the right literature openly available. Unfortunately many of the books written specifically for teenagers are disagreeably moral in tone, but there are nevertheless many books which tell teenagers factually what they want and need to know about physical development, sexual behaviour, marriage and childbirth (some of these are listed in the bibliography). Teenagers will often be too shy or embarrassed to ask for them if they are not displayed on the open shelves. Librarians who issue these books only on request do so to reduce the risk of defacement by prurient youngsters, but this is a risk we must take. We should be able to feel that a teenager who wishes to learn more about this important part of his life can do so without formality at his local library, and we should certainly not add to his embarrassment and uncertainty by restricting the books, as though they dealt with improper subjects.

SELF IDENTIFICATION

Another hurdle which the teenager must successfully negotiate concerns his ability to find his own correct place as an individual in society, rather than remain one of a featureless mass. Sometimes, in order to assert his individuality, he will reject the adult world and its standards completely, although total rejection is comparatively rare.

In addition to developing some perception of himself, the adolescent at the same time realises that there is a type of person which ideally he would *like* to be. The latter is not specifically a characteristic of adolescence, and self-identification with particular ' heroes ' of fact or fiction is indulged in by most children from quite an early age. It need not necessarily be harmful, as it can encourage the child or adolescent to strive toward certain ideals in order to emulate his hero. In many cases it is neither harmful nor harmless, being a purely fashionable identification with an actor, actress or pop star. The subject of admiration might perhaps be a famous athlete, patriot or worker for humanity, in which case much good can result. In a few cases the teenager might choose a hero whose powerfully evil attributes appeal to him—such as Hitler or de Sade—and we must be thankful that this does not happen often. A further point to remember here is that at the time a child or adolescent is building his personality on a model, he is passionately keen to learn all he can about the person concerned, whether the character be real or fictitious, and this influences his reading habits.

As a person matures, this identification of himself with virtually unattainable goals tends to diminish, until on reaching adulthood he comes to accept himself for what he is and realises that as an average human being with the normal quota of faults he is still acceptable both to himself and to society.

RELATIONS WITH HOME AND AUTHORITY

The home is a powerful factor which influences a child's psychological development and attitudes. He may, for example, come to rely too greatly upon the control and comfort afforded by his parents, and thus find difficulty in thinking and acting for himself as he grows older. Alternatively, if parental control has been so rigid as to induce fear, this may breed rebellion in the adolescent years and emancipate him from home influence to a greater degree than is desirable or necessary.

The ideal home is one with an atmosphere of developing parent-child co-operation, where parents allow their children as they grow up to assume increasing responsibility for themselves. In this atmosphere the adolescent, while normally making his own decisions, should always feel free to turn to his parents in times of particular crises for encouragement and advice. In this way the natural progression is for parents to become, in the adolescent mind, not so much an authority group but rather friends to whom one can turn.

Many parents despair of their teenage children, and not unnaturally. Because of his rapidly changing ideas and attitudes, his openness to innovations, as against parental orthodoxy, an adolescent often feels that he is on a different 'wavelength' to his parents and finds communication with them difficult. This results in the perennial complaint from parents that they just cannot 'talk to' their children, and the children feel this mutually. In addition, as children spend more and more time away from home with their own agemates with whom they can communicate freely, the home can seem to become little more than a place for eating and sleeping. At this stage the wise parent will realise the advantages which the child is obtaining from his social contacts, rather than assume that he has lost all interest in the security of the home.

The average teenager changes in his attitude towards authority as he becomes an adult himself. The authority groups have the power to make the child and the pre-adolescent dependent upon them. Yet even young children defy the authority of parent and teacher by deliberately misbehaving, for the realisation of the existence of 'them' and 'me' is not purely a characteristic of adolescence. It is with the coming of adolescence, however, that this self assertion becomes more regular. Authority often regards the adolescent as rebellious and destructively wilful because of his acts of self assertion, and no doubt there are occasional examples of this; in most cases, however, the adolescent does no harm during his progress to adulthood, and far from rejecting his parents he still thinks of them as experienced friends who will be on hand when he requires assistance.

LEISURE: GENERAL

It really seems incredible in view of the multitude of ways in which the teenager must develop mentally and physically, that he should have time to spare for leisure activities. Such activities, however, are not merely ' time-killing ', but offer a valuable aid to intellectual and cultural growth, at an age when the teenager possesses a fantastic amount of enthusiasm and energy. Thus his interests will pass, during early adolescence, from one ' craze ' or ' fad ' to another, until in late adolescence he has settled for the few hobbies which really interest him.

The pace of modern living, and the existence now of media of communication which were unknown a few decades ago, leaves less time for the pursuit of those individual interests which can be described as ' hobbies '. There are more opportunities today for the teenager to enjoy comparatively passive leisure activities such as the cinema, radio and television, and although these media are influential sources of ideas it may be that teenage crazes for, say, stamp collecting are not as prevalent as they were in former decades.

It is obviously useful for a librarian to know how the normal teenager's interests and activities develop and change over the period of adolescence from a passionate interest in many activities to a more adult selectiveness. In compiling the following brief notes the present writer's constant source of reference was Gesell's standard work on adolescent psychology (listed in the bibliography). For a more detailed breakdown the reader is referred to the book in question.

Early adolescence—Interest in childish things disappears. Many new interests found: pets; mechanical things such as radio, making models, car and plane spotting (boys); photography; arts and crafts such as drawing, writing, music and needlework (girls); reading, including newspapers and magazines; a keen interest in sports, participating even if not a good player.

Middle adolescence—Boys still keen on sports, although more emphasis placed on personal prowess; girls losing interest in sports; girls display more inclination toward social gatherings rather than indoor hobby interests; pop music, collecting records; reading becoming more selective, and social life leaving less time for reading; for the mechanically minded, a continuing interest in radio and working models; a developing interest in part time and full time employment.

Late adolescence—Impossible to categorise; choice of activities a more mature, personal, individual thing rather than a question of following the group.

LEISURE: VISUAL MEDIA

The main entertainment media, television and the cinema, and to a lesser degree radio, are regarded by many people as a primary cause of the adolescent's apparent loss of interest in book reading. This is certainly true, and will be discussed in the next chapter, but what concerns us when examining the psychology of adolescence are the reasons why young people like these media, not the reasons why they dislike reading.

To young people in the second half of the twentieth century a world without television is inconceivable. In spite of the fact that it is still a recent invention, it has made sufficient impact to have progressed well beyond the provision of entertainment programmes (if we may admit of the question) to pass the long winter evenings. It clearly gives young people something which books are unable to give them, because to some extent they prefer to watch television rather than to read.

Firstly, television aids the adolescent in his social development in two ways. Whereas he can watch television in a social gathering at a friend's home, perhaps along with others of his peer group, it is hardly possible for the same group simultaneously to read and therefore share a book. Chatting about the programme, or even about something other than the programme, is frequently more important than the attention given to the programme itself. Thus television affords the adolescent an opportunity, or perhaps even an excuse, for a gathering of the gang. It also presents the current social scene in the widest—indeed most international —context. Social development is one of the most important factors of adolescent psychology, so these points are in favour of television.

Secondly, television offers the watcher a means of escape from his problems, and characters with which he can identify himself.

Books can also offer these things, but with its imagery television can do it more credibly and more easily. With visual images the viewer does not have to exercise intellectual imagination to create a situation or character, as he does when reading a book. Having read a book, the teenager can only identify himself with his interpretation of the mannerisms and behaviour of his hero, unless the author's descriptive powers are of a quality and objectivity which few authors possess. The television hero, on the other hand, is a visual being whose physical characteristics, hair style and mode of dress are there to be emulated individually and communally by the teenagers who idolise him.

Thirdly, the adolescent mind is an enquiring mind, and television offers information in a way which teenagers find interesting. The teenager's inclination to hero worship also makes him interested in all the current activities of his hero of the day, be he footballer or pop star; by the time these activities are reported in book form, if in fact they come to be reported, they have lost their topicality and the teenager is no longer interested. True, they are reported in the newspapers, but television is still more appealing than newsprint in the way it shows the hero ' live '.

Not all young people see a conflict between television and books, however, and fortunately there are many adolescents who do not regard these two media as mutually exclusive. There are two sorts of television viewer—the selective and the nonselective. The selective viewer does not experience a conflict between television and books because he draws on both for his inspiration and pleasure. The nonselective is invariably a person whose imagination is incapable of creating fantasy for himself as credibly as television does it for him.

These same factors also apply in lesser degree to the cinema. As with television, the cinema provides an opportunity for mixing with one's peers or dating a boyfriend or girlfriend. The cinema also offers character images with whom the adolescent can identify himself. When we turn to radio, however, we find that the attraction is quite different. Without the visual element of the cinema and television, and the descriptive element of literature, what has the radio to offer? Simply sound, which is a commodity modern youth apparently cannot do without. Silence means boredom and solitude to many young people, who are naturally gregarious and whose creative imaginations are perhaps dulled by over-exposure to the pre-formed images of television. Disregarding the educational and informational content of radio, as most teenagers get this from television anyway, the chief attraction is its simulation of some other form of human presence when the teenager is alone. This is surely demonstrated by the solitary teenager walking down the street with his ' transistor ' glued to his ear in full and noisy spate, although some people do hold that this is just another instance of social defiance.

The adolescent, then, obtains certain things from television, cinema and radio which he is unable to obtain from books. Thus to a certain extent the use of these media is advantageous to him. But what of the much discussed harmful effect on the young mind of some of the more horrific and sensational offerings of television and the cinema? Does this have a bearing on the development of personality? This is a study in itself which can only be covered adequately in a full length book, but as an aspect of adolescent psychology it must be briefly mentioned here.

Firstly, it can not be denied that many film and television presentations tend to 'glamorise' sordid and violent areas of human activity. A particularly violent type of thriller may be seen and enjoyed by millions of people of all ages, and will probably stimulate a desire for more productions of the same type, although it is unlikely that more than a handful of the viewers will regard it as other than fantasy entertainment. With the possible exception of young children (who because of programme planning in the case of television, and film certificates in the case of cinema, will generally not be in a position to view) it is extremely doubtful that the general audience will see the story as offering real life situations to be emulated. A few adolescents may identify themselves with the evil characters, perhaps even modelling their behaviour in some way upon them, but if this happened frequently we should have received more evidence of it.

Secondly, it is argued that the opponents of television violence have confused cause and effect. That is to say, they contend that watching violence on television causes a teenager to commit violence; whereas it is equally feasible that a teenager with a tendency to commit violence watches television violence because of it. Does this therefore exonerate television, if it feeds the warped mind rather than creates the warp? Finally, it is coming also to be argued that prolonged exposure to such phenomena as television violence have a progressively ' callousing ' effect upon the viewer, but research on this question is not far advanced.

Although the common contemporary view of the teenager encourages us to believe otherwise, one teenager can be as much an individual among his agemates as can one child or one adult. Therefore he will possess likes and dislikes peculiar to himself, and this applies as much to his reading tastes as to his tastes in other respects.

It is inaccurate, therefore, to generalise completely on the subject of teenage reading interests, but there are certain defined categories in which young people are particularly interested. Stories of adventure and exploration, for example, provide the adolescent with heroes who have overcome great obstacles and faced considerable dangers. So too do the folk myths and sagas. Romantic novels, in which the young heroine generally manages to solve her emotional crises and make a happy marriage, can be a comfort to adolescent girls who are disturbed by similar problems. These are just two examples of reading categories with character building potentials which are frequently underrated.

Books can offer the adolescent assistance in his development principally by giving him some insight into his own problems. If the adolescent regards himself as emotionally or physically ' odd ', which is by no means uncommon, reading about other adolescents can give him the reassurance he needs. Other types of book can help him in his relationship toward adults; or tell him, for example, how another person grew up to become financially independent with a family of his own; or teach him social, racial and religious tolerance; or give him particular information about the world which his enquiring mind demands; or else just entertain him so that his emotional problems take second place, if only for a short while.

A comprehensive study of adolescent reading interests has not been made for some considerable time. Although rather outdated in some of the specific titles it lists, George Norvell's *The reading interests of young people* remains the standard work on this subject; it was published in 1950, the result of a twelve year investigation into the reading of high school students. For a detailed study with comprehensive lists of books and other reading matter to illustrate the findings, present readers are referred to this book. Briefly, however, it has been established that three general factors noticeably affect the reading choices of adolescents:

Firstly, sex—boys and girls seldom have been found to like the same book. Whereas girls prefer books containing a liberal amount of sentiment and romance, boys prefer books in which action and male characters predominate with no trace of effeminacy. In late adolescence there is not such a marked difference in reading tastes between the sexes.

Secondly, age—reading interests change as an adolescent grows older. Norvell found that the change is gradual rather than rapid, and that a book which is enjoyed by a person of one age will usually be enjoyed by someone two years younger or older, which leads to the conclusion that one cannot label a book specifically for, say, ' thirteen year olds '.

This brings us to the third general factor—intelligence. Bright children go more rapidly through the normal progression of reading interests than do slow children. Again, this makes it impossible to categorise a particular book as suitable for a child of a specific age.

The principal intention of this chapter has been to identify the salient points of adolescent psychology, in order to demonstrate its bearing upon librarianship. If we are to serve the teenager, and to approach him in the right way, we must know something about him. To cover the subject adequately requires a book of considerable proportions written by an acknowledged expert in the field. For the reader who wishes to go more deeply into the subject than has been possible here, several such books—all of them standard works which the present writer has found invaluable—are listed in the bibliography.

CHAPTER TWO:

The reasons why

Is there a 'teenage drift' from libraries? Surprisingly enough, and in spite of ample evidence to the contrary, there are librarians who dispute that the drift actually exists. There may be isolated cases of libraries which are well used by the local teenage population, but these are inexplicable exceptions which can probably boast more good luck than good service.

Various reports and investigations in the United Kingdom have revealed that the 'average' teenager has little interest in reading books and using public libraries. The problem is nothing new; the *McColvin report* commented upon it in 1942. The *Crowther report* (1959) stated in paragraph 171 that 'over half the modern school boys and girls interviewed . . . had at one time belonged to a public library; only sixteen per cent still belonged after leaving school'. The *Nuffield survey*, which was made in the university library at Leeds, showed 'that some students taking special studies have managed to avoid borrowing a single book from the library'. In a report sponsored by King George's Jubilee Trust, and compiled by Pearl Jephcott in 1954, it was shown that in one area only twenty four of 159 young people held a public library ticket, and in another area the figure was twenty five out of 129. The survey conducted in West Sussex by H K Gordon Bearman in 1961 showed that over ninety per cent of the teenagers questioned had belonged to a public library; over forty per cent at secondary schools and approximately twenty five per cent at grammar schools had ceased to use the public library by the time they left school. Details of these reports are given in the bibliography.

From this we may conclude that the problem has been with us for some time, and that it is not so much a result of our contemporary society and its many nonliterary attractions as we are given to suppose. The boom in the mass media, which today influences young people away from reading to recreations requiring less intellectual effort, receives most of the blame for the present situation. It is obviously part of the reason, but if McColvin noticed a teenage drift in 1942 there must be other factors which existed then and which, indeed, still exist today. These factors indicate a failure by librarians, by teachers and by parents.

Why do many young people reject the public library on leaving school, or in some cases earlier? The main reasons which can be identified are, briefly, as follows, although it must be remembered that some teenagers—albeit the minority—manage to overcome these factors and use libraries continuously.

Firstly, the use of books other than those prescribed for examination purposes is in some cases likely to cease when teenagers embark upon their GCE or CSE years at school; moreover, many teachers possibly do not actively encourage wide reading at this academically vital stage. Assuming that teachers were to give this encouragement, this in itself might be a danger—many teenagers already regard libraries as an integral part of education (and thus to be abandoned on leaving school), so in advocating general reading a teacher might unconsciously be linking school and public library even more, to the potential detriment of the latter.

Consider that a boy or girl must work consistently hard to pass 'o' levels, then perhaps 'A' levels, followed sometimes by a college course or vocational training; add to this the organised sports and extramural activities which he or she is expected to endure; plus the recreational activities and pleasures of which most teenagers are only too pleased to partake (some probably in protest at their regimentation within school and college); small wonder, then, that their frequent cry is not 'I have no interest in reading' but 'I haven't the *time* to read'. Libraries are being crowded out of their lives.

Another reason for the teenage drift is the allegedly 'middle class' atmosphere of many public libraries. Perhaps 'formal' would be a better word to describe this. It is hardly surprising that young people, who are at an age when informality is preferred, should decide not to use an institution with such an aura about it. This formal atmosphere is not only apparent in some library buildings, but also in the stock and the attitude of the staff.

Younger children using the junior library tend not to notice this atmosphere so much, and in addition they have the benefit of trained children's librarians. When they reach the age of twelve or thirteen, in some cases when they are younger, the influence of the children's library appears to weaken. Readers of this age begin to feel too old for the junior library and too young for the adult library—another reason for the drift.

At this stage, even before considering the factors of today's commercialised society and the attractions of the mass media of entertainment, it can clearly be seen that there are long standing reasons why teenagers abandon public libraries. Teachers (some, not all) are blameworthy because of their concentration on standard textbooks and literary ' classics ', and their failure to emphasise to their pupils that reading in its widest sense is really nothing to do with school and examinations. Librarians (some, not all) are blameworthy because of their preservation of the library's formal atmosphere and their failure to make special attempts to provide a service to teenagers.

Parents, too, are blameworthy, although in the majority of cases they are not aware of the harm they are doing. They are responsible for the teenage drift from libraries insofar as they do nothing to influence their children to become or remain readers. Many teenagers see no books at home, because the parents do not themselves read anything besides newspapers. Some parents will encourage their children to read in order to help them with their education, but this does not assist the children to continue reading when they leave school—in fact the opposite is the case. In addition, the home atmosphere is often not conducive to reading; non-stop television or radio, the rule in many homes, is a hindrance to the young reader, who may not even have a room of his own where undisturbed reading is possible. And finally, sadly enough, some parents feel that private reading is an unhealthy and antisocial trait for their children to be exhibiting.

Another factor which affects the use of libraries by teenagers is their awakening interest in the opposite sex. Well before leaving school, and certainly to a considerable degree afterwards, a large proportion of their time is spent dating, dancing, and mixing with girl friends and boy friends. Reading is a more isolated and therefore less attractive pastime, and it is natural that teenagers should devote a smaller part of their time to it. But it might be said, if they are interested in sex, surely we can offer them the material relating to this interest? Of course we have books on sex written for teenagers, but most librarians will agree that many teenagers are not impressed by them; teenagers prefer, naturally enough, to discover these delights for themselves, and are quick to realise that so many books strike a high moral tone which seems designed to discourage them. We do, however, provide contemporary novels which deal in a way they understand with relationships between young people. If they require them, we have them; if they do not require them we must accept this, for it would be unwarranted of us to insist on playing our part in this personal aspect of their lives.

In any case it is apparent that while many young people find little time to read because of increased time spent with members of the opposite sex, they sometimes resume their reading habits when they have settled down to married life. Once they find themselves with the responsibility of a home, there are numerous subjects on which the library can supply them with information. Thus we may lose them during the ' dating ' years, but later they return to make use of the services which the library has to offer.

Finally, there is the influence of the mass media. We blame the producers of records, films, radio, television and trashy magazines for our problem far more than we blame librarians or teachers. This is, perhaps, not really fair; the products of the mass entertainment industry are with us, they are fulfilling a purpose, and most of the people behind them are in business for honest profit with no intention of depraving or corrupting youth.

We must remember that from the age of about twelve young people become conscious of a wider world; the world outside the confines of school and the home. The discothèque, the bowling alley and the cinema are all attractive parts of this world; within the home itself there is the escape of television and the record player. Teenagers have money with which to enjoy all these pursuits, and the added pleasure of enjoying them with members of the opposite sex. They prefer group activities, not a solitary activity such as reading. If they *do* visit a library it is with a group —and they are usually rapidly ejected!

28

Our task as librarians, and the task of teachers, is not to sneer at today's teenage pleasures; they have their important place in modern society. What we have apparently failed to do is to link libraries with them, in order to emphasise that the book is as relevant today as it ever was. If we can convince the teenagers that a library can be as important a part of the contemporary scene as a discothèque, then we might break through.

The fact that teenagers spend their last years at school studying for specific examinations has a serious effect on their general reading. For example, a grammar school student will take 'o' level GCE at about sixteen, but will in many cases reject recreational reading at fourteen or fifteen in order to devote more time to academic studies. This no longer applies to grammar schools only; most students at secondary modern, technical high, and comprehensive schools sit CSE examinations, if not the GCE, and the effect on their general reading habits is noticeable.

In this matter the fault does not lie with the young people themselves, but with the examining bodies, and partly with the schools, for a system whereby examinees may obtain adequate pass marks by relying on the contents of prescribed textbooks. Without using any library, school or public, the young person to whom success in his school leaving examinations is of importance may achieve that success entirely by reading and rereading only the books given to him by the teacher, the same books used by all other members of the class.

Fortunately this situation will come to an end. It must do so, and a revolution in education methods has been brewing for some time. The ideal system will be one in which the most important component will be the library, not the teacher; the teacher will guide students through their courses, will encourage them to read freely and not restrict them to set texts, and will then leave them to it. This method, self directed learning, has been discussed for some time now, and is of course general at university level, and if adopted by schools in the future it can do much to demonstrate to students the relevance of libraries. Certainly we shall not then hear that cry of the student which makes all librarians weep 'I have no time to use libraries, as I'm studying for my GCE.'

The educational practice known as a 'project', which is a type of self directed learning, involves the teacher awarding pupils a subject and then leaving them free to discover for themselves all they can about it. Most junior departments of public libraries receive visits by hundreds of children in the course of any month, searching for material relating to their projects. There is, however, one practical danger in this. If (as often happens) the teacher fails to contact the library to ensure that there is sufficient material available on these sometimes specific subjects, then the children may be disappointed and frustrated when the library is unable to offer them anything. Close co-operation between teachers and librarians ensures that children on projects find that the librarians have been able to anticipate their demands and ensure that sufficient material is available. Let us hope that such basic co-operation will be universal by the time every level of school pupil is engaged on self directed learning.

Another way in which schools may encourage their students to widen their reading habits during their examination years is by including in the curriculum more time for current affairs, and for such general topics as appreciation of the mass media. It is important that young people should realise that teachers and librarians do not condemn all the offerings of the mass media; schools could do more to show them that libraries, education and the popular arts are all part of one world. Books such as *Understanding the mass media, Culture and environment, The popular arts* (and others which are listed in the bibliography) suggest topics for study and discussion. Perhaps if more time were devoted in schools to studying these important facets of contemporary society—for example, the press, advertising, the cinema—it might encourage young people to become more liberal in their reading.

So far we have been discussing methods of widening the non-fiction reading of the examinee teenager. Fiction, however, has a place here also. This is a convenient point at which to mention literary ' classics ', which have probably been responsible for influencing many young people away from reading. Compulsory reading of standard classics, particularly for examination purposes, has long been a feature of school life. Fortunately, the practice is declining, as to most teenagers these books are boring, require an unnatural degree of concentration, and offer them little intellectual satisfaction or enjoyment. To many of them must occur the thought ' If this is reading, I don't want any more of it '. But as far as general and contemporary fiction is concerned, many students of history, geography, science and the arts (to give but a few examples) can learn about their subjects from novels, and perhaps enjoy the experience of reading them. A good historical novel may be as useful to a student of history as a prescribed textbook. If more fiction reading were advocated in schools at this stage, this would help to send teenagers to the public library.

The situation is changing, however. More teachers are adopting a liberal approach to their study of English literature, and the examination syllabi must surely follow suit eventually. The new CSE syllabus for English literature certainly includes works which students will derive more pleasure from studying than those rigidly set by the examiners of the past. Undoubtedly much contemporary literature is worthy of study, and since work in class should lead to better literary appreciation and the enjoyment of good books, it is clear that this liberalisation of the English syllabus can do immense good. Considering that most of the students who become habitual readers will probably consume a higher proportion of fiction than any other category of book, the amount of school time spent discussing fiction will obviously not be wasted.

It must be borne in mind, however, that a teacher who gives his students encouragement to read widely and to use the library service runs the risk of harming the cause which he is supporting. At least this is so with the teenagers who, having received this encouragement from their teachers, assume therefore that education and the public library are inexorably linked. The end of school days, they feel as a consequence, are also the end of public library days. Thus it is easy for teachers and librarians to think that 'we can't win'; if one fails to persuade students to read widely, they stick to the basic textbooks and need not visit the library, whereas the teacher's encouragement to read widely associates the library too closely with the school. We also come up against the fact that some young people who do not get to grammar schools believe that in a way they are social failures, the result of the present British system of separating goats from sheep at the age of eleven. To cover this, they sometimes strike an attitude of nonchalance and declare that anything connected with education is 'square' or 'cissy'. Too much library publicity from their teachers can certainly result in them neglecting libraries for recreational as well as educational purposes. What, then, are the teachers to do? There is no definitive answer, except that they must continue to advocate liberal reading and the use of libraries, while at the same time taking care not to labour the point.

Another factor worth more detailed consideration is the sentiment expressed by some teenagers that the public library is a ' middle class ' institution. By this they mean that the general atmosphere, stock and, presumably, staff of many libraries is more acceptable to middle class (or even middle aged!) readers. It is, to an extent which few librarians would be prepared to admit, quite true.

Take, for example, the state of the premises in which many authorities have been providing library services, in some cases since the turn of the century. No doubt they will be replaced by new buildings when they eventually fall to the ground, or at the earliest when they are condemned as unsafe. New buildings, of course, cost money—and present day standards do not always represent money well spent—but until local authorities realise that library architecture needs to be brought up to date, the majority of buildings will never attract the majority of young people.

If a teenager plucks up the courage to cross the imposing threshold of one of these gloomy institutions, he may often find the interior equally forbidding. On every side he is faced with instructions not to smoke, not to talk, not to bring in his dog or perambulator, and not to spit (assuming he wants to do so). In more ways than one, he sees the writing on the wall and departs!

Some librarians, too, fail to make the newcomer—especially if he is a teenager—feel welcome. There are many library assistants who are only too prepared to indulge in interminable conversations with Mrs Robinson, who comes in three times a week for her 'Agatha Christies'. While Mrs Robinson, it must be quickly added, deserves an unbiased amount of personal attention, so too does the teenager. But teenagers frequently complain, when questioned in surveys, that members of library staffs are unfriendly towards them, or that they display apathy and give insufficient help. Here let me hasten to say that I refer to British libraries; the United States has a tradition of forceful library service to youth of which she can be justly proud, and which we in this country could usefully strive to emulate.

Not all library assistants can, of course, force themselves to 'like' teenagers, although a considerable improvement in public library staff training programmes would be useful in teaching staff how to create better public relations with all sections of the community. The ultimate answer lies in appointing specialists as youth librarians, a topic which will be covered in the next chapter.

It is not only the professional staff, however, who sometimes possess an unfortunate manner when dealing with teenagers. Commissionaires and porters, who usually include among their duties a responsibility for maintaining law and order within the library, can be particularly officious when faced with young people. Although their natural exuberance sometimes needs to be kept in check, teenagers will not respect an institution whose servants embody an attitude of petty authoritarianism.

There are other aspects of libraries as official institutions that young people do not like. Some consider that a two week loan period (still in force in many libraries) is inadequate. Fines act not as a deterrent to keeping books overdue so much as a deterrent to using the library at all; and if they were abolished (which many librarians would surely like to see happen), young people might correspondingly feel that we were more interested in encouraging them to read than in taking their money. Rigid age restrictions between junior and adult departments are another example of library officialdom; so too is the limitation of the number of tickets which each reader is allowed.

To summarise, if we wish to attract and retain teenage readers the officious 'middle class' atmosphere of public libraries must disappear. We must prove that libraries do not exist only for the well educated or for the seekers after education; that we do not delight in penalising or excluding young people whose demeanour we do not personally like.

A significant failing connected with the 'official' nature of public libraries concerns the feeling of some teenagers that they are too young for the adult department and too old for the junior department. Here again it is the formal nature of the library which is at fault, if it has created an arrangement whereby teenagers must either remain in a department which is 'just for kids', or else transfer immediately to one of a scope and arrangement which is overwhelming to the average teenager. With most libraries there is no middle way, no special department to serve those of intermediate age.

Even though most libraries do not provide separate facilities for adolescents, this is no reason why adequate books should not be provided which are designed and displayed to attract the attention of young people. Many of the books stocked in adult departments are not written specifically for older people; but young people can be so bewildered by the shelf arrangement, and (in some cases) lack of help, that they cannot find them. In the matter of display we have much to learn from bookshops, record dealers and supermarkets.

In view of prevailing criticisms that libraries are only for the middle aged or the very young, should we make more attempts to cater for the special interests of adolescents? The answer is a modified affirmative; modified because many young people have no special interests, but show a liberality of interests as marked as the average adult. Of course there are a few subjects (pop music, careers and youth hostelling are examples) which are specially interesting to teenagers, and we must provide plenty of material concerning them. But there are many more subjects (such as sports, fashion and automobile maintenance) which are of interest to all sections of the community, including teenagers, and books on these topics would be eagerly read by young people if only they could find their way to them on the library shelves.

Finally, there is the question of books written specifically for teenagers. Sad to say, they are almost nonexistent. Not all teenagers are capable of proceeding direct from children's books to those written for adults. What is needed are authors who will write nonfiction which is geared neither to university level nor to the young child, but to the average secondary school leaver; a few nonfiction series do this, but not many. Similarly, most adult fiction demands a degree of concentration and a vocabulary which some young people find themselves unable to muster, although they have progressed beyond junior fiction. Between the two there exists a need which authors and publishers should be satisfying. We should now be seeing the production of novels specially written for the teenager, which would have two effects. Firstly, it would give the less educated teenager alternative reading to the comics and paperback trivia which is the only matter available to him today; and secondly, he would no longer feel that

the library has nothing to offer him which is neither ' too old '
nor ' too young '.

The mention of paperbacks and printed ephemera brings us
again to the mass media—that inevitable part of contemporary
life, caused by two revolutionary phenomena, the dissemination
of sound, pictures and print on a non-exclusive scale, and the
emergence of ' pop culture ' which created the body of teenage
consumers. Scientific progress made the mass media possible; the
increasing affluence and the habit of filling of leisure time with
recreation requiring little intellectual effort, traits frequently
exhibited by teenagers, will ensure that the media not only
flourish but expand. Our problem is, do we consider this a cause
for concern? Have libraries of books still a role to play in this
world of reproduced images and sounds?

The answer, of course, lies in the fact that while the influence
of libraries is considerably less powerful to the young mind than
is that of the mass media, the young mind is itself in a transitory
stage. One cannot blame young people for wanting to escape in
their leisure time from the world of the classroom into a world
which appears to be the essence of everything that isn't boring or
regimented. Some books, of course, are themselves a form of
escapism, and as librarians we presumably believe that escape
into good literature is qualitatively more satisfactory than escape
into the world of pop music. What we need to realise, however,
is that although an adult equates literature with escapism, many
teenagers find reading a book hard work. There is a conflict
between the occupations of reading—an unsolicited activity which
requires positive effort and which the home and educational
atmosphere seldom encourages—and the mass media, which are
automatically and forcefully available because the essence of these
media is that they have to solicit a committed audience, so that
their blandishments are active and, for the undiscerning, hard to
resist. Thus many young people, when faced with this conflict
between reading and other forms of entertainment, choose the
latter.

Those who completely condemn the modern media as a deterrent to reading should firstly seek to understand what they are
condemning. The cinema and television, for example, are not
completely divorced from reading. They fulfil the function of
reading in many respects, by giving information, or educating,

or just by telling a story—and many teenagers prefer these media because they require less effort on the part of the consumer and can be enjoyed by a group, whereas reading is a solitary activity. We must also recognise that films and television can in their turn create a demand for books by stimulating the viewer's interest in the works of a specific author after one of his books has been dramatised; similarly, we know that reading can be affected by educational broadcasts on television and radio, and this has been found in a recent survey reported by Luckham and Orr in the *Library Association record*. Television and books can and should co-exist in this age; so much so that a television set should be standard equipment in every library. Those who criticise young people for watching television or films should bear in mind that many adults pursue interests which have nothing approaching the quasi-educational content of the mass media— such as whist, football and bingo—and are chastised far less for doing so.

Another point to bear in mind is that when we accuse teenagers of a lack of interest in reading we are not being strictly correct. They read, some of them avidly, but are not particularly interested in *books*. There is a distinction to be drawn between reading —that is, absorbing the printed word—and reading *books*, which is using a specific form of presentation. Teenagers read their local newspapers, for example; many of them read daily and Sunday newspapers; they read magazines and comics; and some of them read paperback novelettes. So the only task is to show them that there are other things worth reading. It should be an integral part of secondary education.

In what way can schools help to show that the offerings of the mass media are but one part of communal life? Mainly by educating their pupils to appreciate and critically appraise quality —to learn to distinguish between the good and the bad. General study sessions, as advocated earlier in this essay, can cover this useful ground. Radio and television could also be used in schools rather more than they are today; at present they are used mainly for schools broadcasts, but they could be used at other times to provide the pupils with matter for discussion. In this way their appraisal of programmes might become more enlightened.

Courses dealing with the cinema, television and radio can be valuable in demonstrating that these are art forms. So is the book.

If young people are taught to link these media in their minds, to discuss their likenesses and differences, their relative merits and demerits, they might then begin to understand that the book is just as important a facet of the contemporary scene as are the other media.

This chapter has attempted to outline the main reasons for the teenage drift from public libraries, and to comment upon them. It has not been its purpose to suggest remedies, although these are sometimes implicit in the comments. Methods by which the drift might possibly be decreased will be discussed in the following three essays. It would be wrong to close this discussion, however, without mentioning two factors relating to younger children which to some extent have a bearing on the problem under discussion.

Firstly, although we are examining the period of adolescence, we should be wrong to concentrate all our efforts and attention purely upon this age group when attempting to solve the problem. L R McColvin, in his report of 1942, which revealed him as one of the most perceptive and far-seeing librarians of his time, made the following statement: ' The real reason why we lose children is that when we do we have never really had them, because their use of books is superficial, apart from and not part of their constructive interests '. Insufficient efforts are made by librarians to attract and secure children when they are very young; the standard of service in some junior departments is still too low, and opportunities are lost at this valuable stage when children are more susceptible to teaching and less diffident in asking for assistance. It is a point worth considering that an improvement in the stock, staff and advisory service of a junior department will make it a more pleasurable and useful place for a child to visit; and, if only in the case of a small minority of teenagers, the pleasures of adolescence will perhaps not entirely overshadow the influence of their period in the junior department. So there we have a reason for the teenage drift that we *can* do something about—the fact that some teenagers did not receive satisfactory service while using the junior department, and so did not acquire the library habit.

Finally, there is the question of school libraries. Are they a help or a hindrance? In certain respects they can be both. The improvements of recent years in school library facilities, and the inclusion of first class libraries in many new schools, are an encouraging sign that education authorities are becoming aware of the need for good libraries as an integral part of the process of learning; thus they are a distinct help to children while they are attending school. As school libraries improve, however, so they become more self-sufficient, even to the extent of satisfying the children's demand for fiction; this means that more children in the future will find their school libraries adequate for their reading needs, and will consequently be at a loss when they leave school. If this situation is to be avoided, some line of demarcation will have to be drawn in school libraries. Should they, for example, stock fiction? Teachers will need to give pupils more encouragement to use school and public libraries as supplements to one another. And, in the end, there is and will be a greater need for close co-operation between public libraries and schools than ever before.

CHAPTER THREE:

Organisation and staffing

If we have decided that a child should be enabled to progress smoothly from the junior to the adult library, what must we then do to bring about this transition? Many librarians, it must be admitted, do nothing; they do not accept that special intermediate provision should be made for the adolescent, and believe that the gap between the two departments will be bridged by anyone who really wishes to do so.

Our task as librarians, however, is not to create two widely differing departments, and then expect a young person for whom neither department is specifically intended to find his way without our help. We already know that many teenagers consider themselves to be too old for the junior library; the stock, the approach of the children's librarian, and the general atmosphere of many junior libraries are naturally geared to the seven to twelve age group which is the backbone of the department's readership. Similarly, teenagers are too young for confident use of the adult department; the classification, cataloguing, range and size of stock is confusing, and adequate readers' advisory services are not always readily available. It surely follows that some method of separate provision for adolescents is desirable.

There are three main methods by which special facilities may be offered. They all have their frequently voiced advantages and disadvantages, some of which are discussed below.

1 SECTION IN THE JUNIOR LIBRARY

Advantages: Theoretically this method need incur no extra expense to the library, which is a potent argument in a local government department. If it is to be effectively staffed and promoted, however, some extra expenditure is inevitable.

Some children are reluctant to leave the junior library; if they stay, even after they reach a suitable age to transfer to the adult library, the adolescent section will provide them with suitable

39

material. A section in the junior library will cater only for those who *wish* to stay. Advanced readers will transfer anyway.

The possible 'stigma' of the junior library is removed, as it would now contain works by adult authors such as Agatha Christie, Hammond Innes and Elizabeth Goudge. Thus a teenager will not feel that it is a department catering solely for the younger child, and will at the same time be given an introduction to some adult authors.

The children's librarian can guide readers from the time of their enrolment at primary school age until their transfer to the adult library, and would have suitable books to offer them at each stage. But is this possible in practice? The time of the children's librarian is normally fully occupied with younger readers, and this may result in adolescents being neglected.

Some younger children with advanced reading ages will be able to use the adolescents' section if it is part of the junior library.

Disadvantages: What happens when a teenager has tired of the section? There are no other books in the junior library which would interest him, and there is still a gap between the junior and adult libraries. The chance that he will not transfer therefore still remains.

In spite of the addition of adult stock, some teenagers will continue to regard the department as a junior library, and will not use the section. They will be those who dislike mixing with younger children, and feel discontent because their pretension to adult status is thus demeaned.

The younger children tend to be noisy, which is frustrating for the teenager who wishes to use the section for study purposes.

A junior library which provides material for teenagers may tend to encourage an immature child to remain too long, preferring to stay rather than to transfer to the adult library.

Books from the adolescent section can be borrowed by young children and there may be parents who will object that adult material is openly available in a department intended for juniors.

2 SECTION IN THE ADULT LIBRARY

Advantages: Again in theory, no additional expense need be involved. But again in reality some expenditure will be necessary on staffing.

The section would provide books suitable for teenagers which, if in the junior library, might be objectionable to the parents of younger children.

The transition to the adult library would be simple. They are, in fact, already there, within the department and surrounded by the books which they will be using in the future.

Teenagers can, if they wish, easily use both adult and adolescent stock.

An assistant in charge of the adolescents' section can be responsible for integrating the readers within the main department, and can deal with senior school classes.

Disadvantages: Rumbustious teenagers in the adult library may be criticised and resented by adult readers—and staff!

It may not, in fact, be possible to provide a member of staff to be responsible for the section.

If adolescents are free to use the adult collection without supervision, they may borrow material which is undesirable or morally harmful to them. (But it may be argued equally convincingly that to deny them access to sections of the adult stock is to add to the enticement of those sections.)

3 SEPARATE INTERMEDIATE DEPARTMENT

Advantages: Teenagers prefer to have their own department, where they feel more relaxed and where there are no adults to criticise them. Exactly the opposite view is held by some librarians, however, who maintain that teenagers do *not* like to be treated as a special class.

There is scope for a full time youth librarian, who can devote his energies to his readers and introduce them to the adult library at the appropriate time.

A separate intermediate department provides the space for extension activities specifically aimed at teenagers, and study facilities are also possible.

Disadvantages: The establishment of an intermediate department creates two gaps instead of one. It does not wholly solve the problem, as its readers still have to be introduced to the adult library. But, ask its adherents, are not two small gaps preferable to one large gap?

It can be an expensive drain on resources. Extra accommodation and staff are required, and books which are already stocked in the adult and junior libraries have to be duplicated.

The intermediate department attracts only readers who wish neither to remain in the junior library nor to join the adult library (unless membership of the intermediate department is made a compulsory step). Bearing this in mind, is its expense justified?

From the statements generally made in support of, or against, the various methods of library provision for teenagers it may be seen that many of the pros and cons cancel one another; for many of the advantages of each method there are corresponding disadvantages which lead more than ever to an inescapable conclusion— that the only feasible course of action is to consider the individual merits and demerits in relation to each library service and its local circumstances, and then to make a decision.

In short, after prolonged and repetitive discussion over many years, there is no completely right or completely wrong method of providing library services for teenagers. The only wrong decision is to ignore the problem and not provide any adequate facilities whatsoever. The problem is clear cut: public libraries are not reaching a large section of the community. To combat this, two essentials exist; firstly, to introduce a method of separate library provision, no matter which method is chosen; and secondly, to appoint or allocate to staff the specific responsibility of organising services to youth. These two essentials are the subject of the remainder of this essay.

THE ADOLESCENTS' SECTION

An adolescents' section in either the adult or junior department of a public library is comparatively simple to establish. These sections can require little in the way of organisation and administration, and perhaps for this reason many librarians are already providing this type of service in their libraries.

They normally take the form of a few shelves, with a label attached to signify that the books are of special interest to ' Teenagers ', ' Young adults ', ' Under twenties ' or some similar designation. It is doubtful whether all the books shelved in these sections in many libraries are of ' special ' interest to the readers for whom they are intended; in fact, unless someone is given specific responsibility for maintaining the section it can soon become a depository for adult literature of a juvenile standard and for children's literature which is considered too advanced for the junior library. This means that the section is not fulfilling its function, which is to offer a selection of books to those teenagers who require it which will help to bridge the gap between the junior library and the adult department. To do this, the section must include suitable books selected by a librarian with genuine interest in the purpose of the section, although he may be a general assistant given this responsibility. It cannot be emphasised too strongly that stock maintenance in a small section is just as important as in a separate intermediate department, if not more so; the staffing requirements will be discussed later.

No special rules, regulations or formalities should be necessary in these sections. Holders of either junior or adult tickets may be free to use the section at will, and, similarly, no teenager should be compelled to use the section if he prefers to transfer directly between the two departments. The section exists for no other reason than the convenience of those readers who require it. Separate application forms and tickets, or any other routines which will give the section unnecessary autonomy, are therefore unwarranted and wasteful.

The adolescents' section must avoid setting up yet another barrier to the young people. It must fit into the general library organisation, and its function is to act as a co-ordinating service linking the adult and junior libraries. The duties of the assistant will naturally have to be varied according to whether or not he has full time responsibility for the section, but his main tasks will be to introduce young people to his section and to the full range of services available in the entire library.

The number of books to be included in the average section is not likely to be sufficient to require a separate book fund. Many of the books will not need to be ordered for the adolescents' section specifically, but may be selected from the stock arriving in the adult and junior departments, provided that the selection is carried out carefully. This operation involves complete co-operation between the three librarians concerned, in case it may be argued that the assistant is poaching on the resources which the adult and junior departments are creating with their own book funds. Against this, it may be said that as a certain percentage

43

of the registered readers in the existing two departments are teenagers, and some of them will want to use the newly formed adolescents' section, the assistant is justified in taking some books from each department's allocation in order to build up his stock. Co-operative book selection is the only answer, preferably through regular meetings at which the assistant can make it known which titles ordered could usefully be allocated to his section. On arrival, the books need to be marked in a distinctive manner so that they do not find their way back into adult or junior stock.

By building an adolescents' section with new books, and increasing its size and scope by transferring from the existing stock of the other departments a reasonable number of books suitable for teenagers, the establishment of an adolescents' section need involve no additional expense. If it is to be efficiently organised, and promoted by means which will be described later in this book, it may be necessary for an extra member of staff to be appointed. That it requires little or no additional money to establish the section, may account more than any other for the fact that many librarians in Britain have selected this method of providing a service to youth; and for that they cannot be blamed.

THE INTERMEDIATE DEPARTMENT

Despite the disadvantages of a separate intermediate department in a room quite distinct from the adult or junior library, many libraries have used this method with success. They have not been adopted to any marked degree in Great Britain, but a large number of public libraries in the United States have established intermediate departments and found them worthwhile.

We have little practical experience of such departments in Britain, but tribute must be paid to the excellent work which has been done in Walthamstow (now incorporated into the London borough of Waltham Forest). As far back as 1924 Walthamstow pioneered the idea of a service to youth as a separate self-contained unit to bridge the gap between the junior and adult libraries. Today the youth library service in Waltham Forest is still continuing its success; service takes the form of a separate room in the central library adjacent to the adult lending department, and at branches there are youth sections in the adult lending libraries. Aimed at readers aged thirteen to seventeen,

44

the central youth library is under the control of the central lending librarian and operated by specially selected members of his staff. Readers in the thirteen to seventeen age group have distinctive tickets but all readers of any age are free to use junior, youth or adult departments at will and restrictions on freedom of choice are reduced to the absolute minimum. Transfer is thus a gradual and not a sudden process and the staff of the youth library in the course of their advisory work make use of the adult stock whenever appropriate. Youth members are not charged fines for keeping books overdue, regardless of whether they are borrowed from youth or adult departments. The adverse criticisms levelled at intermediate departments are many and varied, but the idea certainly seems to work in Waltham Forest. It is fulfilling the obligation which every library has—to provide adequate library facilities for teenagers—without inflicting unnecessary restrictions upon the young readers.

If the method has been successful in Waltham Forest it raises the question of why so few other British librarians have established intermediate departments. The main drawback is probably the perennial library bogey—expense. Whereas a small section for teenagers can be set up without extra funds for books, and at a pinch without specially appointed staff, a separate intermediate department normally requires both. The potentially high initial cost of building up the department, and the necessity of appointing a youth librarian on a departmental head's scale of salary, have made the idea impracticable to many librarians who might otherwise adopt this method of providing attractive facilities for teenagers.

In general, consideration should only be given to establishing an intermediate department in the central library of a municipal system. Young people tend to congregate in town and city centres, and it is reasonable to suppose that if such a department exists they will not wish to travel an unnecessarily severe distance to use it. Provision for young people in branch libraries can be made by means of adolescents' sections. Similarly, in county libraries it would probably be impossible to set up intermediate departments in branches, although consideration should certainly be given in the bigger branches or regional libraries which serve large populations.

One general rule in administering an intermediate department is that no library routines should be carried out in the department which result in the staff having less time for their special duties. If it can be arranged, the departmental staff should not spend a large amount of time processing books (which really should be done by the general accessions or processing department), or writing overdue postcards (which could well be the task of the adult library staff). These are merely two examples, but when planning the work of the intermediate department it must be remembered that its staff, presumably small, should be available as much as possible to introduce new readers to the facilities and to act in an advisory capacity.

Eric Leyland, in his book *The public library and the adolescent*, suggests that time-saving ideas and devices should be constantly tried in order to leave the departmental staff free to carry out their more important duties. To ask readers to replace their own returned books on the shelves, for example, may be a practice frowned upon by some librarians; but, as Leyland points out, its value in an intermediate department lies in the time saved for the assistant and in training the young readers to find their way round the shelves.

The routines that readers are expected to undergo in order to join many of Britain's libraries are too complex and formal. In an intermediate department this just will not do. Young people detest formalities and what they regard as unnecessary ' red tape '. They should not be required, for example, to obtain a guarantor's signature on their application forms; although they are not registered on the electoral roll and do not pay rates, we should be prepared to demonstrate our trust in them. Our risk is not so great in terms of irrecoverable books, and by introducing unnecessary safeguards we may be dissuading many young people from using the library.

The question of how many tickets to allow is one on which no clear rules can be formulated; rather is it a matter for the local authority to decide. Some flexibility is advisable, however; it is unwise to issue certain tickets for nonfiction use only, but preferable to issue a number of general tickets. If this is done, the readers will have further welcome evidence that the library does not tie them down.

Fines could be abolished in the intermediate department, for they can be a reason why young people stop using libraries. Anything resembling 'punishment' is undesirable. If fines are replaced by a tactful mention—not a lecture—that the retention of books is unfair to other readers, most teenagers will understand and remember for the future.

Hours of opening are another matter to be arranged by the local committee. Here they have guidance from no less an authority than the *Albemarle report*, which suggested that the growth of teenagers' interests will be greatly encouraged if public libraries remain open until ten o'clock on at least some nights of the week. The implementation of this would undoubtedly arouse staff opposition, but libraries do not exist merely for the convenience of the staff. It is, of course, easy to use this 'pat' phrase, but sooner or later it will be taken as fact. In addition, it should be borne in mind that most of the intermediate department's readers will be attending school or working; hours could be modified in view of this, but the department should always be open during lunch hours and school holidays.

Statistics can be another vexing problem. In this department's case, as in any other library department, the best plan is to keep statistics to a minimum. If the departmental staff spend much time on compiling their various statistics, this represents a loss which could be better spent on dealing with readers. The other disadvantage of statistics is that too often they represent an end in themselves, and little use can be made of them. The library committee will, however, require occasional evidence that the newly formed intermediate department is not a white elephant, and most committees can be told everything they need to know if three statistics are maintained for the department: number of registered readers, number of issues, number of books in stock. These figures will also be necessary to calculate the proportion of the book fund which should be devoted to the department.

STAFFING

As mentioned previously, whatever method of library provision is established for teenagers, it is desirable for special staffing arrangements to be made if the service is to be efficiently organised and promoted.

In large municipal systems there is ample scope for the appointment of a youth librarian. In the United States he would normally be termed a 'co-ordinator of services to young adults', and this

47

describes his work more accurately; his function is not only to supervise the intermediate department at the central library, but also to act in a co-ordinating and advisory capacity for the whole system. Appointments of this nature could usefully be introduced in municipal systems in Great Britain, as specialists are needed to assume full responsibility for work with teenagers; the existing children's librarians would thus be released to devote more time to the younger age group.

The youth librarian should be on the same professional basis as other departmental heads, in terms of salary and direct responsibility to the chief librarian. He must be in a position to co-operate closely with the superintendent of branches, if one exists, and would need to maintain good relations with all branch librarians; the latter is vital, as branch librarians must be given no occasion to feel that the youth librarian is conducting unwarranted interference with any branch services to teenagers. It is the task of the chief librarian to decide where specific responsibility lies, but in general the youth librarian should have no need of any control over matters at branches, although he should be able to advise, criticise, comment, and eventually aspire to see an improvement in branch library facilities. The youth librarian should formulate general plans for the youth services in the system, and the chief librarian should ensure that they are agreed with the superintendent of branches.

It is obvious that the youth librarian can spend little time at individual branches, and to ensure that the overall standard of service is raised and maintained it is necessary for an assistant at each branch to be given specific responsibility for the adolescents' section. This will not, at the smaller branches, be a full time responsibility, but it is vital that as much staff time as possible be given to editing the stock of each section, introducing readers to the service and acting in a readers' advisory capacity. Promoting the services to teenagers for the whole system, and contact with outside bodies, may be left to the youth librarian at the central library. In larger branches, some of which might even have their own separate intermediate libraries, much more can be done at a local level by the assistant concerned. If the existing staff structure at branches is inadequate to allow one assistant to spend even part of his time on maintaining the adolescents' section, consideration will need to be given to increasing the establishment. However difficult this may be, it is essential that the standard of service to young people be raised and kept at a high level.

Smaller municipal library authorities may not consider it necessary to appoint their own youth librarians, if even in the central library they are only able to provide a section rather than a department. An assistant should, however, be given responsibility for the section; although the assistant may be on the establishment of the adult or junior library, he should be allowed to cross the boundaries of any department which he considers necessary to provide services to his readers. He should be free to take readers into any department, to help them choose books or to introduce them to the staff or services. This sort of personal attention is often preferable to leaving a teenager to his own devices; too often the door to the street outside lies between two library departments (metaphorically speaking), and the teenager might take that door if left to find his own way.

County library systems present their own individual problems in this field as they do in many others, but in general the staffing situation may be approached in much the same way as in large municipal systems. The only differences which substantially affect the issue are the larger geographical areas covered by counties, and the fact that it may be unnecessary to set up an intermediate department in the headquarters library. The problem of covering a large geographical area has already been solved in many counties by regionalisation, and for many administrative purposes these regions have become virtually autonomous. There are aspects of the library service which should be supervised for the county as a whole, however, and one of these is service to youth.

All county branches should provide some sort of adolescents' section and an assistant who devotes all or part of his time to maintaining this service. All regions of counties should have a regional youth librarian. All counties should employ a county youth librarian, who should be responsible for the entire county and act in an advisory and co-ordinating capacity with the regional youth librarians. This means that the existing organisers of work with young people, who already have a considerable volume of work to perform with the younger age group, should not remain responsible for direct services to youth.

Appointment: It is generally agreed that one of the most important components of a library's services to youth is the person chosen to administer them. The right person must be selected to fill the post of youth librarian, and no less important are the assistants given the task of organising the adolescents' sections in branches. In the latter case, rather than leaving the choice completely to the branch librarian or superintendent of branches, recommendations should in addition be considered by the youth librarian; it is, after all, his own sphere of the service which is going to be improved or damaged by the person chosen at each branch.

The basic qualities required of an assistant with special responsibility for youth are:

1 A knowledge of what teenagers like and dislike,

2 A knowledge of books. The adolescents' section, perhaps more than any other section of the library, must contain books which are of proven appeal to its readers. There is a chance that if a teenager finds an entirely unsuitable book on his shelves he will mistrust the section thereafter and may even stop using it altogether. Not only is a knowledge of adult literature required, but it should be remembered that the reading ability and interests of teenagers are so wide that the assistant will also need a thorough knowledge of children's literature. He must therefore be himself widely read, especially in fiction, and must be able to relate his knowledge to what teenagers like—and avoid selecting for himself rather than his readers. There must be no personal censorship, and no exclusion of certain authors if it is known that their books are enjoyed.

3 A considerable enthusiasm for the job, and the energy to carry it out. No assistant who lacks interest and feels that he is being pushed into a deadend job will do the job efficiently.

4 The strength of personality and of will to deal with any situation likely to arise. Teenage readers will not respect a weak assistant who becomes flustered. With this we may bracket the strength of will to control the unruly element. It is possible that an older assistant would be preferable, particularly as teenagers may expect a very young assistant to be no more knowledgeable about books than they themselves. It must be emphasised, however, that if strength of will and personality are too evident the assistant becomes the 'typical' librarian of our public image; this should be avoided, and a pleasant personality in addition to firmness is required.

5 A modest knowledge of adolescent psychology; this may perhaps help the assistant to realise when tact is advisable, or to understand his readers' problems, but too much reliance need not be placed on this point when selecting assistants. If the appointed assistant is not conversant with adolescent psychology, his knowledge of the subject will rapidly improve after a few months in the job!

6 A genuine interest in teenagers, an uncondescending manner and a sense of humour. Lack of these in an assistant means that he is most unsuitable for work with teenagers.

7 A knowledge of bibliographical tools and how to use them. The ability to compile booklists is also a valuable attribute.

8 An acquaintance with the local senior schools curricula. As many teenagers remain at school until they are eighteen, the assistant should know what books they might require for educational purposes.

9 The ability to relate teenagers' interests, which are varied and rapidly changing, to the resources of the library. This implies a reasonably thorough knowledge of the stock of all departments.

10 Finally, the basic idea of an adolescents' section is to prepare the readers for the adult department, so the assistant should be prepared to regard each reader as a transient in need of gradual introduction to the complete world of books.

These, then, are the main qualities which should be found in the assistant with special responsibility for the adolescents' section in branches of a municipal or county library. The youth librarian, or in a county the county and regional youth librarians, should also have these qualities, but because of the co-ordinating aspect of their work they should possess the following additional qualifications:

11 Previous library experience should be as varied as possible, bearing in mind that in contact with outside organisations the librarian will be required to answer questions on many features of the library service. If he is well versed in library work in general, he will also find it easier to win the support and co-operation of other heads of departments.

12 Some ability as a public speaker would be of advantage, as the youth librarian will be expected to talk on library services to groups and outside bodies. Not only must he have the confidence and ability to speak in public, but he must be able to speak

in an interesting and forceful manner so that his audience feels that the library really has something to offer.

Duties: The duties of an assistant responsible for the adolescents' section in a branch library have already been briefly covered. He will have little time to do more than act as a readers' adviser.

The intermediate department in a central library should have an assistant available to staff its counter at all times, as on many occasions the youth librarian will be absent from the building, maintaining contact with outside groups.

The youth librarian's duties should include the following:

a) The general supervision of library services to teenagers in the area which he covers.

b) Advice to readers, which he should perform from a separate desk in the intermediate department; at times when he is not available for this work, a second assistant should relieve him on the desk. The youth librarian should spend as much time as possible in the department, however, as it is only by dealing directly with the teenagers themselves that he is able to keep informed of their interests and needs.

c) The development of services. To this end, monthly meetings of all members of staff responsible for work with teenagers can help in formulating future policies.

d) The arranging of book displays in the intermediate department, at schools, youth clubs, colleges and other centres. Assuming that branch librarians prefer to retain responsibility for arranging displays in their own branches, the youth librarian will be able to advise them on any which are specifically aimed at teenagers.

e) The compilation of book lists, which will be distributed to young readers at all service points and will be of value to staff in their work with teenagers.

f) Visiting schools, colleges, youth clubs and other outside establishments for the purpose of promoting the library service.

g) Giving advice to branch librarians in their extension activities with teenagers.

h) Selecting the books and periodicals for the intermediate department and, depending upon local policy, either selecting the stock for adolescents' sections at branches or advising branch staff in their selection.

i) Training the assistants who have been allocated to work with teenagers in the branches and in the central library.

j) If a special classification and cataloguing scheme is used in the intermediate department, the youth librarian may carry out this work during his periods on the enquiry desk, but a large amount of the work may be delegated to his assistants. If no special classification and cataloguing scheme is used, the books may pass through the main cataloguing department in the normal way.

k) Arranging lectures and extension activities in the intermediate department.

l) Deciding which of the duties listed above he must perform personally, and delegating others to his assistants.

m) In short, the youth librarian should be guided in his duties by the pre-eminent need to stimulate the interest of young people in the library as an educational and recreational centre, to bridge the gap between the school and the public library, and to improve the library services to young people.

Similarly, most of the duties listed above would apply to each regional youth librarian in a county, assuming that there is an intermediate department in each regional headquarters library. If there is no department, the regional youth librarian will need to spend some time at various libraries in the region to make his personal contact with the young people.

Training: There are no paper qualifications available for library service to youth. The only British Library Association examination which touches on the subject to any noticeable degree is the Final List B paper on 'Library work with young people'. As this paper concentrates on services to younger children, however, it is true to say that any chief librarian who intends to appoint a youth librarian will have no applicants with paper qualifications indicating a theoretical knowledge of work with teenagers. Perhaps some day the appropriate paper will be introduced into the examination syllabus, but until then a chief librarian must look for a chartered librarian who has the personal qualities listed earlier. Then it becomes the responsibility of the youth librarian to train all staff responsible for work with teenagers.

In-service training should cover book selection and appreciation, the organisation and administration of an intermediate department, and all special procedures related to work with this age group. Sessions should be devoted to adolescent psychology, possibly with lectures by experts. Finally, time should be spent on instructing the assistants in one vital aspect of library service—public relations. They must know the correct method of dealing with readers; this is something every assistant must be taught, and practise constantly, to ensure that the welcome accorded to young visitors to the library attracts them to return.

CHAPTER FOUR

Co-operation with other agencies

A library is not adequately fulfilling its purpose in the community if its readership consists entirely of those who are normally avid library users and need no encouragement to come. It is necessary to attempt to attract those who need extra encouragement and incentive to use our services, because (let us admit it) we are paid to do so; and we are failing in our duty as librarians if we are apathetic and sluggish in this matter. The adolescent section of the population contains comparatively few avid library users, and therefore it is of paramount importance not only to establish a service which will meet their requirements, but also to create and use our opportunities to attract those teenagers who consider that the public library has little relevance in their lives.

This essay, and the next, will deal with various ways of 'promoting' the public library service. We can attract and retain readers by the use of extension activities and library publications, which form the subject of chapter five, but first of all we must realise that the disregard which many teenagers show for the public library can not be countered by the library working alone. We need to co-operate with various outside bodies; with their help we can make a greater impact, and achieve more success in our campaign to gain the interest of young people.

Sometimes the help which springs from such co-operation is rather one-sided; the library gets most of the benefit. It is not always so, however, and often the librarian can be as useful to an outside body as that body is to him. In any case, the only consideration should be that the teenagers themselves derive the maximum benefit. Any organisation connected with youth which is reluctant to co-operate with the library should remember this fact.

THE SCHOOL

The public library and the school are, as has been stated on numerous occasions, natural allies. At least some of our aims

55

are similar, the main one being that we are attempting in our different ways to provide intellectual substance which will not only satisfy the normal child's natural curiosity but will encourage him to want more.

There is a problem, however. Whereas the public library seeks to turn a child into a habitual reader, and thus help create the adult reader of the future, the aim of the school (or at least of the school library) is to concentrate mostly on the present. The school librarian or head teacher who obstinately refuses to have any connection or co-operation with the public library usually does so because he considers his school library to be self-sufficient, and in many schools, particularly the new ones, pupils can most certainly satisfy all their reading needs. But what of the pupil when he eventually leaves school? If he has previously received no encouragement to use the public library, he is unlikely to begin to do so at school leaving age. On the other hand, if he has been using the public library throughout his school career it is conceivable that he will continue to do so. This is something which librarians and teachers really need to get together and discuss.

A great deal needs to be done, therefore, to convince many teachers of the need for greater consultation and co-operation between the public library and the school. The blame for non-co-operation, of course, does not lie entirely with teachers; some librarians are equally diffident in making contact with their local schools. Again, the situation varies from one library to another; county libraries, which until recently were grouped with schools under the county education officers, may have found it easier to achieve co-operation because of this, and consequently many counties have enjoyed fruitful library/school relationships. There remains much more to do, however, and in order to reach the adolescent it is particularly important to build up a close co-operation between libraries and secondary schools; much of the past progress has been made with primary schools.

It is not proposed to spend a great deal of time here in recounting the various ways by which public libraries and schools may co-operate; most of it has already been said before. Instead it may be more relevant to examine the features of co-operation which have a direct connection with the age group under discussion, and which are designed to solve the two main problems of teenagers in relation to libraries: that they do not know what we offer, and do not know how to use our facilities.

Firstly, it is obvious that many young people are unaware of what the public library has to offer. Ours has never been a profession to sound forth with metaphorical trumpets in order to advertise our services. Consequently, many people have little knowledge of the public library other than as a purveyor of recreational reading for the middle-aged, or as a place where other people can read the daily newspapers in enforced silence. And teenagers have been known to show pleasurable surprise when they enter the library for the first time and find that we do have something of interest to them.

We must devise ways of telling the teenager about the facilities we have available, and this should be the sole purpose of the class visit to the library and the librarian's visit to the school. Many librarians have for some years been inviting classes of school pupils to visit their libraries, and the content of their sessions has varied considerably according to the enthusiasm and personal views of the librarian concerned. For example, some classes have received talks on the physical makeup of the book, on simple historical bibliography, and on the development of libraries. This type of thing is most interesting for the librarian, but probably evokes little genuine enthusiasm in the adolescent audience, and is certainly irrelevant as a method of getting young people interested in their local library.

Classes of pupils from secondary schools should most certainly be invited to visit the library, and the librarian responsible for services to this age group should visit the schools in return. These are inherent and vital components of our work with young people, and a complete programme should be devised by all librarians. But the programme should be carefully pruned to exclude items which do not fulfil the one and only purpose of such activities: to give information about our facilities and how to derive maximum benefit from them. The actual content of such talks must be decided by the individual librarian, because this depends to a large extent upon local circumstances, and upon the existence of any special services which school pupils need to know about.

Basically the sessions will include introductory talks describing the various departments of the library and what they have to offer, but in order to make this more interesting for the audience the general descriptions need to be followed by a certain amount of ' embroidery ' and practical work. It adds meaning to the sessions on ' how to find a book ' and ' obtaining information from reference books ', for example, if they are followed by practical exercises. Visual aids can be used to supplement the talks; in fact, each talk should be interrupted at various points in various ways, so that it does not become monotonous and cause the audience to feel that they might just as well be in school.

Talks to school pupils, whether given at the library or at the school, should also be used by the librarian to bridge the gulf between the public library and the school library. For too long they have both been treated as autonomous units, with many teachers whose pupils have access to a good school library adopting the attitude that there is really no need to use the public library at all. We must emphasise in our talks to young people that the public library and the school library are inter-related; that the school library, while often catering adequately for their educational needs, does not offer the range of material which the public library offers; that in order to satisfy their out-of-school interests they require the public library as a supplement. These are points regarding which the public librarian should not be a lone voice; the school librarian, and the teacher, should be emphasising such points to their pupils equally firmly.

There are other methods of co-operation which should be adopted between school and public library to ensure better likelihood of pupils reading widely while they are at school, and maintaining interest in the public library after school leaving age has been passed. The better ideas stem from a personal and friendly relationship between the youth librarian and the local school librarians, and the following are suggested:

1 The youth librarian and school librarians should co-operate in the compilation and production of special subject booklists. They should be distributed as required to readers at the public library and school libraries.

2 Arising from this, readers at the schools should be encouraged to go direct to the public library for their books, rather than rely on the public library lending the books to the schools, as this will ensure that young people receive an opportunity to discover what the public library has to offer.

3 Co-operation can include the planning and staging of exhibitions and displays, to be held in the schools; again, this will give teenagers at school some of the information about the public library which they require, in addition to drawing their attention to the various categories of book which the school library is unlikely to have in its stock. The books should be carefully selected in order to cover the subjects in which young people are interested, and should reflect out-of-school interests rather than the academic curriculum.

4 The youth librarian, bearing in mind that he wishes his department to be used to some degree for educational as well as recreational purposes, should maintain continuous contact with head teachers and school librarians so that he knows the syllabi and can anticipate demand; he must also make it known that he welcomes young people to the public library for research and ' projects '. Teachers themselves should be encouraged to warn the youth librarian well in advance when a large number of students are likely to descend upon the public library in simultaneous search of material on the same subject; if this is not done, the students may find the library wanting and, as discussed in chapter two, this could discourage them.

5 The importance of renewed efforts to acquaint young people with the public library when they are in their final weeks at school should be realised by teacher and youth librarian alike, as the difficulties of reaching some teenagers after they have left school are enhanced. If earlier in their school careers they have attended talks by the youth librarian and been taken on class visits to the public library, they should receive a brief ' refresher ' before leaving school; the most satisfactory theme of this would be to demonstrate how the public library can aid them in their future careers and further education. In addition, information supplied by the schools concerning their ' leavers ' will enable the youth librarian to send brochures and booklists to them. It can not be emphasised too strongly that if action is not taken at this stage it may be too late.

6 Teachers can be of considerable help in publicising to their students the various types of extension activity which the youth librarian organises, and which will be discussed in the next chapter. Some activities, such as literary discussion groups, can be held in the school itself.

7 Finally, a general point: in order to co-ordinate the efforts of the youth librarian, the school librarian and the teachers, a joint committee should be formed so that communication is facilitated and policies for youth library work may be formulated.

These are just a few means by which library and school may work together to attempt to ensure that the use of the public library becomes an agreeable habit for young people which they will wish to continue after leaving school. Many librarians will know of other methods of co-operation, often quite original, and it would be useful if these could be brought to light more frequently in the pages of the professional journals. The librarian who is genuinely trying to make a place for his service in the crowded lives of local teenagers is always interested to learn of new projects in which both library and school can participate, and he realises the necessity of grasping every opportunity so that young people may be reached before they leave school and are possibly lost to us.

FURTHER EDUCATION

Not all teenagers, however, are completely beyond our reach after they have left school. A large proportion of them still collect together in a formal way, in youth clubs and colleges, for example, and we must use this fact to continue the work we have been doing while they have been at school; in some cases we might break new ground with those who have previously shown little interest.

More young people than ever before attend some form of further education establishment after leaving secondary school. Some of them do this with no particular career in mind, but attend courses leading to further ' o ' level or ' A ' level GCEs; others attend courses connected with their chosen careers, some full time and some on day release. In all these cases we have an opportunity to co-operate with the colleges in presenting to students the image of the public library as an educational force which can help them considerably in their studies, and as a means of supplying them with information concerning their own personal interests.

University students present a special problem, although many of them are not ' teenagers ' and so come outside the scope of this book. It has been found, for example in the *Nuffield survey* at the University of Leeds, that many students make little use of the university library's lending facilities—this presumably indicates that they also avoid the public library, except for study space and reference facilities. The difficulty in this matter is that most librarians would consider it unnecessary to 'push' the library's services to university students. One would automatically assume that supposedly intelligent people of a high standard of literacy and education require no encouragement to use the library service; that they should know the value of our service for educational and recreational purposes. If, as it seems, these are false assumptions, what can we do about it? Not many librarians face this particular problem, as not every town contains a university, but those that need to make more attempts to reach university students could begin by adapting the methods outlined above for work with schools. Some librarians may already have devised ideas to interest students at their local university in the public library, and no more will be said here on the subject because the university student is hardly a 'typical teenager', and it should not be necessary to make the same efforts on his behalf as for the less educated members of the community.

When we turn to further education colleges, however, we find a real challenge which concerns us all. Most public libraries have such a college in their areas, and many of the students who attend them have not been avid readers during their school careers. They are not illiterate—far from it. Their standard of literacy, as H K Gordon Bearman reminded the London and Home Counties LA conference in 1962, is higher than that of previous generations. But many of them have stopped using the public library, for reasons already discussed in chapter two, and while they are together at college we have a worthwhile opportunity of encouraging them to return. Our efforts to reach young people in college rely for their effectiveness upon the youth librarian co-operating closely with the college staff, and in particular, with the college librarian.

At this point let us acknowledge the great advances made in college library provision during recent years, and pay special tribute to that comparatively modern figure, the tutor-librarian. A well stocked and fully equipped library is now generally accepted as an essential part of any proposed new college, although it must be admitted that many of the older colleges contain libraries which are below standard for their requirements.

Nevertheless the situation is improving, and today many adolescents attending colleges of further education have excellent college libraries available to them. In addition, they receive induction courses on library use by the tutor-librarian, who also guides them in their project work and generally helps them to make full and efficient use of the library's facilities. The youth librarian has a valuable ally in the college tutor-librarian; the latter, being a qualified librarian, realises that his students need to know the public library in addition to the college library. The youth librarian, for his part, should acquaint himself with the concept of tutor-librarianship, and obtain a knowledge of how the tutor-librarian works and what he is trying to achieve; there is a useful article by R O Linden, one of the first tutor-librarians, in the October 1967 issue of the *Library Association record*. After assuring himself that he knows the general principles on which the tutor-librarian works, the youth librarian's second step is to arrange and maintain frequent consultation between the two in order to facilitate fruitful co-operation.

Finally, what practical methods exist to promote the public library to college students? With the number of tutor-librarians growing, we can say with optimism that more of this is being done already, and in the future our worries in this respect will have considerably diminished; students will receive encouragement and advice to use the public library. In addition youth librarians may co-operate by using such methods as those outlined above for co-operation with schools. Another technique which has been advocated in the past (by H K Gordon Bearman), but which has not apparently been adopted to any marked extent, concerns the public library supplying collections of books of general (rather than curricular) interest; these can form the basis of displays in the college library, but are more likely to attract attention if they are informally placed at various points about the college for students to examine and borrow if they wish. The main basis of co-operation in the future, however, will be the friendly relationship which should be fostered between youth librarians and tutor-librarians, so that special projects and other 'gimmicks' will be simply 'extras'; if the tutor-librarians, in their contact with students, encourage them to use the public library, this should have more influence than any occasional displays or talks by the youth librarian. There are encouraging signs that this is happening.

YOUTH CLUBS

When considering the position of youth clubs, the problem arises whether a youth club should have its own library, or whether it is sufficient for youth leaders to encourage their club members to read and to use the public library. Arising from this, if a club has its own library, should it consist of a deposit collection of books sent by the public library? These are questions which need to be considered first, for upon the answers will depend to some extent the type of activities which the youth librarian should seek to organise jointly with the club leaders.

The danger which we must avoid if possible is that youth club members, if their club ' library ' is merely a box of assorted books on loan from the local library, should be deterred, by the collec‑ tion's patchiness and inadequacy, from visiting the public library itself; they might consider that if this is the sort of ' rag bag ' the library provides, then the place is not worth a visit. At the other extreme, if there are no books at the club, it will add to the youth leader's difficulty in encouraging his members to read. The club may have its own library containing its own books purchased with its own funds, but that is in the hands of the club itself and does not concern us here.

Ideally, the public library should supply collections of books to local youth clubs. They should not, however, consist of the sort of heterogeneous mixture to suit all tastes which are commonly sent to a prison or old people's home. They should be very small collections, specially selected to appeal to teenagers (this is where the youth leaders co-operate and give their advice), and on arrival at the club should not remain together on shelves in a vain attempt to create a mini-library. A far better idea is to distribute them casually about the club, not only in the ' quiet ' room or study room (if one exists); no attempt should be made to force them on members, who, if they wish, will pick them up unprompted and look at them and borrow them.

Secondly, the main body of book provision between the public library and the youth clubs should be on a specific subject basis. Whereas the small consignment of books mentioned above will be treated as a casual arrangement, and the youth leader should not use them obtrusively to try to engender a love of reading in his members, in the matter of providing subject collections the youth librarian and youth club leaders can together really evolve a strong programme. From reading books on youth club work (for example, the two standard books by Brew and Henriques), it is immediately obvious that the keen club leader organises a tremendous range of activities to cater for the varied interests of his members. Having created a sturdy basis of friendly co-operation between himself and his local club leaders, the youth librarian needs to discover which activities are arranged at which club and when; this done, he should send fairly comprehensive collections of books so that they are on display at the clubs to coincide with the activities themselves.

As an example, let us suppose that on each Thursday evening a youth club drama group meets for play reading and rehearsals. They are at present particularly interested in the works of Pinter, Wesker and Osborne. Next Thursday when they meet, if the youth librarian is doing his job properly and receiving co-operation from the club leader, there will be a display in the club consisting of copies of works by these playwrights, by other comparable writers' books about the modern drama and theatre, and possibly periodicals containing criticisms of these writers' works. The club leader will make it known that the material has been lent by the public library, that the books may be borrowed without formality, that they should be returned to the public library direct, and that if members would like to know more about the ways in which the public library can help them in their leisure pursuits, they are welcome to chat with Mr So-and-so, who is the youth librarian. Be it drama, sports, handicrafts, music or any other activity, the youth librarian should be able to send a special collection of books to supplement it. This method is more likely to get results than a hotchpotch of books supplied as a general deposit collection.

Standards of public library service in England and Wales (the 1962 Working Party report) states in paragraph seventy eight that the public library is making a valuable contribution to the youth service if it brings its facilities to the attention of those who can benefit from them. Apart from the idea outlined above, which certainly fulfils this function, there are other methods. For example, the youth librarian should ask himself these questions:

1 Is it possible for him to visit youth clubs in order to talk about his work, and to give advice in an informal manner concerning reading and the use of libraries?

2 Why not invite club leaders to bring parties of members to visit the library, on similar lines to class visits by schools?

3 Would local youth clubs like to arrange joint activities such as discussion groups and inter-club 'quizzes', to be held at the library?

4 Can he gain representation on local youth councils in order to achieve greater contact with those serving youth and to link youth organisations with the public library?

5 Is he willing to compile reading lists to help teenagers with both work and recreation, bearing in mind that the clubs might be willing to bear at least part of the production cost?

These questions indicate just a few of the ways in which the youth librarian can promote his service to young people through a connection with youth clubs. No doubt the enterprising youth librarian could think of many more.

OUT-OF-SCHOOL YOUTH

Finally, there is the question of out-of-school youth, and more particularly those who are not accessible to us through youth clubs and further education establishments. How can these young people be reached? The short and simple answer is that they cannot, at least by any direct means which can be clearly delineated here. This is because the teenager who does not attend any establishment of further education, does not use the public library, and does not belong to a youth club, is on the whole unlikely to be connected with any other organisation with which the library can co-operate.

This group of teenagers will be dealt with extremely briefly here. This chapter concerns co-operation with other agencies, and with this group there is no agency with which we can co-operate; there is no common denominator which links them together and through which we might contact them. Special activities arranged in the library might attract a certain proportion of them if well advertised and not slavishly linked with books, and these activities are the subject of the next chapter.

Some of them might be reached, however, through:

a) Factories—collections of books at their place of work would serve to draw attention to the library.

b) Shops, which might be willing to allow displays of library books.

c) Churches, whose ministers could provide details of young parishioners to whom the youth librarian could write.

d) The Youth Employment Bureau, for details of teenagers just embarking upon their first job.

e) Probation officers, who might like a supply of books to recommend to their charges.

If the youth librarian attempts to solve the problem of the ' teen-age drift ' from libraries singlehanded, he has little chance of real success. With the help and co-operation of other agencies, he can ensure that his facilities are brought to the notice of many young people in his area, with a reasonable possibility that some will take note and begin to make fuller use of library services.

CHAPTER FIVE:

Extension activities and publications

Although there are three possible methods of providing a library service for adolescents—divided junior department, divided adult department and intermediate department—there is one common factor which should apply, whichever method is adopted. It is wrong to say: 'We have provided the books; now let's leave them to it'. Far too often this seems to be the attitude of many librarians toward their services to adults—they provide buildings, stock and staff, and assume that an effective service is automatically available, when in fact there remains much positive work to be done.

Public libraries are now sufficiently developed, and librarians have become sufficiently free thinking, to elaborate that dangerously simple 'buildings—stock—staff' formula (which must surely have been devised to give the lazy librarian a false sense of security). 'Buildings—stock—staff—promotion' will do for a start.

However, although many librarians do not promote their services sufficiently, tribute must be paid to those who specialise in work with children for the really encouraging efforts which they have made in this respect. Children's librarians seem generally to have an exemplary attitude toward promoting their services, which might well be followed by those serving the more mature sections of the community. It is not suggested, of course, that we hold ' story hours ' for adults! But children's librarians invariably make the sort of effort toward encouraging more effective use of the library and attracting new readers that should be copied by those who are responsible for other age groups.

We are not, however, dealing here with services to adults. As already discussed at length in chapter two, many adolescents show little interest in the facilities we offer, and those who are using our facilities find it very easy to stop doing so. Thus promoting the service—which means taking steps to attract new readers and to keep the ones we already have—is perhaps more important when dealing with this age group than with any other. Promotion is an integral part of a librarian's job, and a responsibility which he shrugs off only at peril to the service he is being paid to promote.

A recent development in Britain has been the much discussed National Library Week. So far this event has been held in 1966 and 1967, and from the viewpoint of 'libraries and youth' these two weeks were not encouraging. Presumably a National Library Week should be aimed at *all* sections of the community, and although reports of the 1966 and 1967 activities showed that many librarians devised exciting and unusual programmes, they were mainly suitable for adults or young children. The adolescent group forms a large part of our public, and more consideration should certainly be given by local authorities to devising events for future National Library Weeks which will show the adolescent what libraries have to offer and how to obtain the fullest benefit from public library facilities. Some programmes did cater for adolescents, it must be admitted, but there should have been more efforts to promote the library to this age group. Libraries in the United States of America regard adolescents as equally important a group as adults or children, and in their National Library Week devote much time to them, and it is clear that some genuine rethinking is required in Britain.

National Library Week, however, is a periodic event. The main purpose of this essay is to deal with continuous ways of promoting library services to teenagers. Libraries in America, many of which have specially organised young adult departments under the direction of a carefully appointed librarian, have devised programmes of continuous reading guidance; the purpose of these programmes is to encourage existing library users to read more widely and beneficially, in addition to attracting new readers to the library.

Firstly, before planning a promotion programme or adopting various methods of reading guidance, it is necessary to decide upon the desirable elements which such a programme should embody. For example, no teenager likes to be treated as a child— they resent it and will probably rebel against it. Thus an activity which is childish in tone, or schoollike in method, must find no place in our programme. Again, the teenager does not like to feel that he is being lectured, which means that while he will accept a talk or activity which is teaching him something in an interesting way, he will most certainly not come again if the technique is oppressively pedantic.

Finally, there are two general points which occur whenever the words 'promotion' or 'extension activity' are mentioned. Should the activities be linked with books and reading, and can we afford to arrange activities which are bound to involve the library in expenditure? The answers to these questions may be rather different when considering work with teenagers, than when considering work with other age groups. On the first question, we already know that many teenagers show little interest in books; if, therefore, we include in our programme some activities which are not directly linked with books, they might help to attract the really difficult ones, and persuade them that the library is not so dead, not so musty, but perhaps even something of a social centre; thus their goodwill toward the library could develop, albeit in a minority of cases, into a greater interest in the other facilities which the library offers.

Turning to the second question, can we afford it? We are talking of the future of the world when we talk of adolescents—they *are* the future, and the better educated they are to face their responsibilities, the more exciting will that future be. Libraries must play their part in preparing today's young people for their roles as tomorrow's adults. Rather should we be asking: can we afford *not* to? Of course any library has a strictly limited amount of money and a scale of priorities on which to spend it, but it must be realised that promotion is not an unnecessary 'extra'; in fact it is wasteful of money to establish good library facilities and then to do nothing to attract more readers. Librarians need to convince themselves of this before they can convince their committees. If the necessary funds are not forthcoming, much can still be done on the shoestring to which most libraries are accustomed, and the majority of the activities described in the following pages necessitate little or no expenditure.

THE TALK

First, let us dispel the feeling that it is impossible to communicate with teenagers. Most difficulties can be overcome quite easily by the correct approach and by subject content which is of interest to them.

Talks to teenagers may be divided into three types: informal, subject, and 'book'. The first type of contact is purely spontaneous, and the opportunity should be taken whenever it presents itself. It is something in which every member of staff can participate, not only the person in charge of services to adolescents. For example, when a teenager asks a member of staff to find a specific book it may be obvious from his manner that he would prefer to learn how to use the catalogue and so trace the book himself; this simple process can be communicated to the enquirer in an on-the-spot chat. If he asks a question about any aspect of the library or its services, the right advice will help the teenager realise that the library is doing its best to assist him to use its facilities to the fullest extent.

The second type of talk is the formal one which deals with a subject other than books or libraries. It is when planning this type that we must remember our overriding decision not to 'lecture' young people. The idea is to plan a programme in which experts will *give* lectures without actually seeming to lecture, and this makes the choice of speakers a particularly difficult task.

Because of the difficulty of obtaining speakers of the right type, the programme of talks should be planned well in advance. If a lecture agency is used to obtain speakers, it is inadvisable to plan a programme according to which speakers happen to be available. The correct course is to decide what topics will interest young people. Youth club leaders, teachers and young people themselves should be asked what subjects they would like to hear experts talking about; from their suggestions a list of topics may be compiled, and a programme of talks devised. Then, having decided upon the subjects to be covered, it is necessary to find the speakers to cover them.

At this point let it be said that local 'experts' should not be relied upon too greatly. Because they are not likely to ask for fees, or at least not large ones, local amateurs tend to be approached far more for their services than acknowledged professionals. The latter, however, are more likely to attract an audience and give the type of streamlined talk which will hold the interest of teenagers and make them feel that the library is alive.

The expense involved in securing the services of experienced professional speakers is worthwhile if they are likely to bring in many young people who have probably never used the library before. This is the main advantage of the 'celebrity' lecture. It is when considering this type of activity that controversy arises whether or not it is the function of the public library to provide pure entertainment, or light educational features, with no direct pressure to encourage members of the audience to borrow books. It is difficult to know where to draw the line, but when dealing with teenagers it is better to avoid using the celebrity talk purely as library propaganda. Accept the fact that your carefully chosen celebrity has brought in the crowds—if this happens, it is an encouraging start—and restrict its connection with books to a small display in the room where the talk is held.

Sometimes a speaker will be willing to mention books connected with his subject—especially if he has written them himself—but it should be remembered that the young people have come to hear the celebrity himself, and will find too many references to further reading distracting. On no account should the speaker be pressured to mention either libraries or books if he does not normally do so within the context of his talk.

The small display of books should consist of volumes in mint or nearly mint condition, preferably in their dustjackets. Young people are not attracted by ancient tomes and they do not share the bookman's delight in fondling the brittle bindings of smelly old volumes. They will, however, handle attractively produced new books arranged in an eye-catching display. They will also, it is hoped, wish to borrow them, and some means should be devised of issuing them on the spot; when the books are returned to the library, the more formal arrangements necessary for becoming a library member can be completed.

There will, of course, be a number of young people attending the talk who are genuinely interested in reading more about the subject, and in these cases the librarian's suggestions will not come amiss. Suggestions for further readings may take the form of short annotated booklists distributed at the time of the talk to those requiring them; the remainder may be placed in the library for any interested readers to take as they wish.

This brings us to the third type of talk—the 'book talk'. The principle here is to encourage readers—and non-readers—to try books by a specific author or on a specific subject, or sometimes to read one specific title. Young adult librarians in the United States have been using the technique of the book talk for many years, and have become masters at communicating to teenagers the enthusiasm which they themselves feel toward a really good book.

The venue of the book talk may be at the library itself, although the audience would in this case be composed principally of those who already use the service, and the speaker would thus be preaching to the converted; this does not destroy the worth of the talk, however, as it may serve to help those existing readers to derive more pleasure from their reading. Other possible venues are the local schools—a ‘captive’ audience—youth clubs and lecture halls.

There is no obvious reason why book talks to young people should not be a regular feature of library practice. To begin with, they cost practically nothing. There is no outside speaker to pay, and unless a hall has to be booked there is little expense involved in arranging the venue. There is a small amount of necessary expenditure—a booklist may need to be produced and distributed to supplement the talk, and light refreshments could be provided to fortify the converted and attract the dubious. The only significant outlay is in staff time.

The success, or otherwise, of the talk depends more on the speaker than on the material. Libraries which have on their staff a librarian specifically responsible for work with adolescents are in a fortunate position here; if he has been appointed because he possesses all or most of the necessary attributes suggested in chapter three, he should be able to give an ideal book talk which will hold the interest and fire the enthusiasm of young people. Librarians who would like to offer talks to teenagers, but who have no youth librarian on their staff, should ask themselves who is the most suitable member of the staff to do the job. It is not always the chief librarian, who may be very good with the Women's Institute but show himself to be a bore and a ‘square’ when addressing a group of teenagers.

Careful preparation is vital. It is necessary first to decide whether the talk will cover a mixed assortment of books on various subjects; several books on one subject; fiction by various authors, possibly on a common theme; or fiction by one author.

Once this has been decided, and a list has been compiled of the books to be covered in the talk, the books themselves should be examined. If time permits, they should be read. At this point the proposed talk would be forming in the librarian's mind, and when he reads the books, the most interesting ways of promoting them will suggest themselves; in the case of fiction, the principal characters and incidents will stand out. The talk itself should not recount the book, merely give enough interesting points about it to make the audience want to read it.

Most speakers, unless their memory and confidence are sufficiently good, will prepare notes to use during the actual talk. The notes may also be kept for future reference when giving the same talk to another group. But it is inadvisable to make obtrusive use of them during delivery; young people prefer the talk to flow smoothly, rather than to hear the speaker reading from a sheaf of paper.

If the speaker can give the impression of an off-the-cuff talk, he will succeed more easily in communicating his enthusiasm for the books he is attempting to describe. The speaker who is obviously thoroughly at ease and fully conversant with his material will command more co-operation from his audience. To achieve this, and so eliminate overuse of notes, it is advisable to rehearse before the date fixed for the talk itself. This will also enable the speaker to time the talk correctly, and remove the necessity of filling time by reading actual extracts from the books—a practice which is not likely to hold the attention of a young audience. The timing should, in addition, be planned to allow for questions and discussion, for distributing booklists and allowing the audience to examine the books on display.

DISPLAY

Having already mentioned display as an adjunct to the talk, it is now necessary to consider it in more detail.

Firstly, to generalise, how are we to interpret the term 'display'? Should we regard it, like Dr Savage in his *Manual of book classification and display*, as including formal classification in addition to specially arranged exhibits? No one can reasonably dispute the argument that books shelved in sequence according to a library classification scheme are 'displayed'; the fact that one book is to be found in close proximity to others on the same subject means that they are 'displayed' for the benefit of the reader who wishes to browse through the available material on that subject. Library display in the accepted sense of the term is something more, however; it is a supplement to the classification scheme. Whereas formal arrangement of the stock may be regarded as a basic factor of librarianship, special displays act as an extra service and at the same time attempt to rectify some of the difficulties which any classified arrangement of books creates for the reader. A display on 'The Elizabethan age', for example, will collect together books from the sections on religion, economic history, science, the arts, social history, and biography; these subjects are distributed throughout the classification scheme, normally shelved in different sections of the library, and their collation in a display thus helps readers.

The term 'display' is taken here to exclude formal classification, which in any case is a subject adequately covered by other works. Apart from any other consideration, if a librarian establishes a separate department or section for adolescents he may decide not to follow a formal shelf arrangement. Rough subject groupings, as used in bookshops, have much to commend them when dealing with teenage readers and a comparatively small bookstock; if this method is adopted, it is even more a part of 'display' than are the formal schemes.

There are various types of display, and it is first necessary for the youth librarian to plan a full programme for some months ahead. Types that immediately come to mind are those consisting of book jackets, of non-book material, and of new books or recent additions to stock. It is with a display devoted to a specific subject, however, that the most exciting possibilities exist; to young people dullness and banality are unacceptable, and it requires a librarian with flair and imagination to produce something which will attract and hold their attention.

Displays should be changed frequently, which is why the programme should be planned well in advance. A list of suggestions for future displays may be compiled and maintained relatively easily by asking the advice of young members of staff and teenagers using the library; their ideas might be surprising in their originality, and will not only be a useful guide to the type of subjects the teenager is interested in, but will provide quite a contrast to the possibly staid and well tried display ideas emanating from the older librarian. Young people could also help by suggesting captions for the proposed displays; snappy titles which will catch the eye and sound alive and up to date are most important if the displays are going to be successful, and young people themselves should be able to suggest ones which might not occur to the more literary minded.

There are other groups to whom the librarian can turn for assistance when he is devising his programme of displays. Local schools, for example, can be most helpful; their co-operation may take the form of allowing displays to be staged in their own buildings, sending volunteers to the public library to help set up displays, or providing material and professional assistance from their art departments. Local shops and societies are sometimes also willing to help; the former could provide equipment to embellish a display on sports, for example, and the amateur photographic society could illustrate a display on photography from the film to the enlarged print. These are just a few examples to demonstrate that a display is more likely to be successful if the librarian does not restrict it to the material and knowledge contained within the library itself; outside help can transform the finished product.

Having planned the programme of displays and decided the time for the first one, what materials are required? Books, obviously, and these should be collected together with due regard to assembling at one point such 'distributed relatives' as those given in the 'Elizabethan' example earlier. In addition to books, one needs display units, tables, some form of backing (pegboard or pinboard), and fittings. If the library possesses no equipment of this type, it is often possible to improvise by 'stealing' a table or two from the reading room or borrowing equipment on long loan from a generous shopkeeper. Glass exhibit cases may also be available, but they should not be used in displays for young people if they are too 'institutional' in appearance. Another necessary part of the display will be some form of lettering; if the library does not possess a set of one of the many ranges of plastic or cork lettering now available, or a set of stencils, or an 'artistic' member of staff who can perform a neat job freehand, the local college of art may provide assistance. There are several comprehensive books on library display listed in the bibliography.

After the books are collected together, and the equipment and lettering arranged, there are still a few more ingredients needed. As only a small part of the library's stock will be used in the main display, it will be useful to issue a duplicated or printed subject booklist so as to advertise the wider selection of books in stock. Then there is the non-book material, such as photographs and maps, which will give the display added variety and create more interest. And finally there are the ' props ', such as sports and camping equipment, gardening tools, working models and mobiles, which, if local shops and organisations are willing to lend them, will add colour and life to the whole effect.

One final point to remember is that the adolescents' department or section will look more attractive if several displays are used simultaneously. The record shops and boutiques which teenagers frequent make expert use of display techniques because the proprietors know that it pays dividends; the shops are full of displays of various types, and they make these places look alive. So in addition to the ' main ' display in a library, there could perhaps be a smaller unit containing novels of adventure, a bulletin board exhibiting new book jackets, various smaller displays of books on the tops and ends of book stacks, in sections of shelving and so on. Far from cluttering the department, a range of displays, frequently changed, will convey the impression that the library really wants to show its wares to the young people just as much as do the shops. We have so much to learn from the professional ' ad man ', and not until we can read a book on commercial display and advertising and know that it is relevant to libraries, shall we be even part of the way to where we ought to be going.

LIBRARY PUBLICATIONS

The various types of talk and display arranged for young people should in most cases be accompanied by a booklist. This is a type of library publication which requires more detailed consideration here, as many examples currently issued by public libraries are not apparently designed to inspire teenagers; they appear to be aimed primarily at the existing ' safe ' library user, and (with some notable exceptions) would not be greeted with any excitement by the younger generation. The public has come to associate the public library service with certain traditions, which may attract older citizens but undoubtedly repel the young. Into our programmes of extension activities and displays we must inject new life, and this is true also of our publications.

Before considering the booklist, which is the main type of publication concerning us here, let us mention the 'guide to the library'. Many libraries issue a duplicated or printed leaflet, copies of which are handed to new readers, sent to local clubs, schools and other organisations, and otherwise distributed to encourage the non-user to use the library, and give the existing library user some facts about the service. Some of these guides are beautifully produced and well written in lay terms, and ideally suitable for the adult reader. More libraries should now consider issuing such guides specifically for the teenage reader, particularly in the case of a library which has an intermediate department or a teenage section of any size.

A leaflet designed for teenagers should have a modern appearance typographically and should include details of the book stock in the adolescents' section, with briefer details of the adult department for purposes of comparison. When compiling the guide, it must be remembered that although it is intended primarily for users and prospective users of the adolescent section, it should also make known the wider aspects of the service; after all, the teenager will sooner or later be thinking of transferring to the adult department, and he needs to know what to expect. Services such as the reservation and interlending schemes, and special features such as the provision of non-book materials should also be covered.

The guide will describe the arrangement of books in the adolescent section, how to find a book, the advisory services available from the assistant in charge, and details of the various extension activities and displays regularly held. Individual librarians will have their own views about what to include and what to avoid, but if it is remembered that the finished product should be both informal and attractive visually, and convey the impression always that the library is trying to help the reader, it cannot fail to have a beneficial effect.

This brings us to the booklist. In the context of work with teenagers it is perhaps better to admit that we are compiling 'booklists' rather than 'bibliographies'. The latter sounds too academic for the field we are considering here, and a booklist sounds much more useful for our present purpose. Again it is advisable, as in all our promotional activities with teenagers, to plan ahead. A librarian who has planned his programme of talks and displays will draw up the booklists to go with them, but in the case of lists which are intended to stand alone rather than to accompany other activities, it is necessary to know exactly what you are going to produce and when you are going to produce it—there is no place for last minute efforts which reveal themselves as such.

Booklists specifically intended for teenagers are a regular feature of library practice in the United States, but few libraries in the United Kingdom have issued them. It is true that many of the excellent lists which libraries produce for adults may be accepted and used to advantage by young readers, but it is surely preferable to design a series of lists of books specially selected for teenagers with annotations which will appeal to them.

Hertfordshire County Library, for example, has done this with *Teenread*. This project, initiated in 1965, takes the form of short lists of new paperbacks and uses the caption '*Buy . . . borrow . . . read*'. It is well printed by HERTIS, and its success must have been due to the attractive appearance of the lists themselves and the obvious pains which have been taken to write annotations which would appeal to its audience. Consider, for example, the following: '*Take two people, one a Cockney mining engineer, the other an English missionary's sister; put them on a river launch in German Central Africa at the beginning of the war, and you have the basic plot of* THE AFRICAN QUEEN. *But C S Forester's story is really the tale of a tub, a filthy, unpainted, thirty foot, flat bottomed launch with an engine so old it is likely to blow its top . . .*' To take another example at random: '*If you want to be a professional teenager and con the oldies all of the time just read between the lines—or even along them—of a book by Colin MacInnes called* ABSOLUTE BEGINNERS . . . *This book jumps.*'

The quotations from *Teenread* show the way in which an annotation can be slick enough (and the term is used here as a compliment) to make a teenager want to read the book. Not every compiler of library booklists can master this technique, but those who can should certainly put it to the fullest use.

So that is the first desirable feature of a booklist for teenagers —snappy annotations, not boring résumés. The list itself should be short if possible, containing a few well chosen titles rather than attempting to be comprehensive. There is scope too for illustrations reproduced from the books themselves by permission of the publishers; again, Hertfordshire has done this in *Teenread*. Another desirable feature is that the lists must look attractive enough to be worth picking up; whereas reasonable effects can be produced with a typewriter and duplicator, if used with imagination, the library which can afford to have its lists printed has a head start. This point may be made when discussing booklists for any age group, but whereas an adult will pick up a poorly duplicated effort because he is interested in the contents, it is necessary to encourage the interest of young people by giving them an appealing visual effect.

The field of booklists for the adolescent is challenging and full of exciting possibilities. It may be a brief list of books on handicrafts or judo, a list of contemporary novels or poetry. If more libraries were to spend time—and, as always, money—on a relatively ambitious programme of publishing such lists, their efforts would surely be rewarded.

GROUP WORK

So far we have been discussing activities in which the library itself is the prime—or only—mover. Talks, displays and booklists are staged or produced by the library, and the teenagers attend or receive them. But there are other activities, in which the audience is not merely an audience but a factor responsible for the very success of the venture. These activities, which if well organised can be rewarding both to the library and to the reader, rely for their success on getting the young audience to participate, and for this reason they will be covered here under the heading of group work. Various types of activities can be arranged by the youth librarian, some of them in conjunction with other local groups or societies.

When deciding on a programme of group activities, a useful preliminary step is to invite a number of young people to form a planning committee. This should result in activities which stand a chance of appealing to teenagers because they are organised by people of their own age. It will also give the teenagers of the community a pride in their library affairs, and encourage them to feel that they are being allowed to use the library in their own way, rather than that a librarian is dictating to them. Thus the committee of teenagers will, with the librarian on the sidelines as a guide, decide on the type of functions they would enjoy; the programme might even be left in the committee's hands for its entire planning and publicity, although the librarian would always be available to give assistance. Such a committee, known as the Youth Council, was formed in Long Beach, California; for an account of its activities, see the article by Doris Watts listed in the bibliography.

The main type of group activity is discussion, where only the subject is laid down and the participants are left to cover it in their own way. Some libraries have tried this with adult groups and achieved varying degrees of success. Many public libraries in the United States have formed teenage discussion groups, and found that if suitable subjects, which teenagers feel strongly about, can be introduced, then the ensuing sessions will be lively and worthwhile. It has also been found that the librarian should if possible keep in the background; the young people will then form their own group, probably elect their own chairman, and organise the projects in the manner they think best.

If the librarian wishes to act as discussion leader, and if it is clear that the group wishes him to act in this capacity, he must bear in mind that his function is not to interfere. His role is to guide and stimulate the discussion. It is possible for him to link discussion sessions with books; for example, to accompany a discussion on education there would be a display and booklist on that subject.

There is, of course, a need for informality. The participants might like to arrange the seating in the way that suits them, and if the library staff are not able to serve coffee it should be made possible for the teenagers to do this themselves.

Another type of discussion is that concerned with books, where young people get together and discuss the books they have read. If the library does not possess the facilities necessary to enable a book reviewing group to meet, this may be done by means of a duplicated review sheet written by young people themselves, distributed at the library and through the other agencies with which the library co-operates. Not only does this type of publication enable those who are interested in contributing to it to find greater interest in their reading, but it also influences to some extent the reading of their agemates. Young people are perhaps inclined to mistrust the titles recommended by an older person, whereas if a book is recommended by a person of their own age it can encourage them to read it.

If facilities exist for a group of teenagers to meet at the library to discuss books, this should be encouraged. It may either be left completely informal, or alternatively a programme of books could be planned by the librarian, so that the participants attending a meeting will all have read the books to be discussed.

The discussion and reviewing of books by teenagers themselves may be given an even wider audience than that likely to be attracted to the library sessions, through the media of radio and television. Public libraries in the United Kingdom have hitherto made little or no use of these media. Much can be learned here from public libraries in the United States, some of which have gone 'on the air' with book discussion programmes by a panel of teenagers. If the resulting programme is of a high professional standard, and if it can be broadcast at a time when teenagers are available to listen, it can certainly dispel any feelings about the public library being old fashioned. Its effectiveness lies in the fact that teenagers (not members of the older generation) are telling other teenagers that they found a particular book interesting, or exciting, or dull, or romantic; and this, one hopes, inspires at least some of the audience to read the book for themselves. This type of project is well worth considering; see Margaret Scoggin's article *Radio's young book reviewers*, listed in the bibliography, for details of how it was done in New York.

There are many other ways in which young people may be brought together in group activities at the library. Obviously not all of them will be interested in current affairs discussion groups, or book reviewing projects, but the librarian working with teenagers will realise that they will be glad to meet other teenagers who share the same interests, in order to discuss and learn more about their particular hobbies. A programme may be planned which, for example, gives one evening to stamp collectors, another to budding writers, another to tape recording enthusiasts, another to amateur photographers, and so on. If it is possible to plan this programme really well, and to allow the young people to organise the evenings themselves if they wish to do so, it will be possible to attract a different group to the library each evening, and these inevitably will include some individuals who have previously not used the library. In addition, it is simple to link the various activities with books unobtrusively by arranging a 'take it or leave it' display and booklist.

To cater for the adolescent who perhaps has no special hobby or interest, more 'general' evenings can be arranged. These may be based on radio, television, music or films, and are worth brief discussion here at the end of this section on group activities.

Firstly, radio and television. One of the advantages of these media as far as teenagers are concerned is that they can be enjoyed in a group, whereas reading is a solitary activity. If a radio and/or television set were installed in a public library for young people to meet and listen to certain programmes, the venture might prove a success. This should by no means be restricted to the so-called 'educational' programmes, as the opportunity to hear or view a cross section of the media's offerings will lead to more fruitful discussion afterwards. This is an activity which, to avoid arguments about the choice of programmes, should be supervised by the staff. There will, of course, be library purists who criticise this sort of activity if it is not linked with books; it is a matter for the individual librarian to decide, but even those teenagers who use the library's 'television room' as a place to come into from the cold are at least setting foot within our walls. There should be books available in the room, and if they show interest in them this is gratifying. If not, we have lost nothing and perhaps gained friends who previously thought the public library something outside their own world.

Secondly, music. This most teenagers enjoy. Music, of course, exists in many forms, and the pros and cons of the classics as opposed to pop does not concern us here. In fact a liking for pop music is no longer considered philistine in enlightened circles. Pop music has become 'respectable', and many of its purveyors are not without intelligence, education or musical skill. Bearing this in mind, a librarian planning a series of concerts can include all types of music without feeling that he is debasing the library as a cultural centre. If he is arranging activities for teenagers, to neglect pop music is to leave a tremendous gap in his programme which will keep much of the potential audience away.

The methods by which music is presented to young people in public libraries must inevitably vary according to the amount of money available. To engage a string quartet, a professional pianist, a guitarist, a folk singer and a pop group can result in a good programme which will attract teenagers of all tastes, but it will cost the library a considerable amount in fees. Although it is possible that local performers will agree to help free of charge, many libraries will be forced to rely upon the tape recorder and the record player. Even without 'live' performers, however, an attractive programme of tape and record concerts can be devised which, while not attracting teenagers in hordes, will bring to the library a number of them who have never been before.

Again one must not be too dogmatic about turning the record concert into an academic or book centred enterprise. Its first purpose is to give the audience an enjoyable evening; they will come to listen to the sort of music they like, and in the case of pop concerts (if space permits) they will probably want to dance. And why not? A display of books will be available for those who want them. Although until recently most books on music dealt with classical music, whereas the field of pop was covered by paperbacks, the increased respectability of the pop scene has resulted in more serious publishers producing books which teenagers would probably be interested to read if only they knew of their existence; the book display accompanying concerts might therefore receive a surprising amount of attention.

Another musical activity which could attract reasonable audiences is the talk and discussion on a specific aspect of music; for example, on the development of jazz, the music of contemporary figures like Lennon and McCartney, the history of operetta, or the story of ballet. There are innumerable subjects which could be covered in this way, illustrated with recordings. Plenty of time should be allowed for the audience to participate with questions and discussion, and with this type of activity a select booklist is always a useful supplement.

Finally, films. The first step which the library can take, assuming it has the facilities, is to invite the local film society to hold its meetings in the library. This might attract a few younger members in addition to older members of the population. A more valuable step, however, would be to give the younger people a film club of their own.

The policy of the library's film club might be merely to show films which are in themselves interesting, and not to make any effort whatsoever to connect them with books. This will certainly encourage the more difficult teenagers to realise that there are no strings attached, and that the library is not 'sugaring the pill' for its own ends. Richard Moses' article, which is listed in the bibliography, describes one such venture under the self explanatory title *Just show the movies—never mind the books!*

Alternatively, it might be decided that the film club must be used to support and promote the library services. If this is so, a series of 'book into film' programmes could be planned, where the film is shown and then discussion takes place comparing it with the book from which it was adapted. This is a project which could be extremely interesting to young people, and might even inspire reading in those who had previously thought it dull.

There are, then, many ways by which a librarian can promote his services to teenagers. This essay has sought to outline a few of them, and it has mentioned some where the connection with books is tenuous. Whether or not a librarian will experiment with these is a matter for the individual, although it seems reasonable to assert that our first step should be to get the young people into our libraries by any means, however unbookish these means might be. The second step is to encourage them once there to make use of the library services, and if they are not interested to refrain from flinging them out on their ears.

The sooner we attempt to emulate the activities of our competitors, the better. Teenagers watch television, go to the cinema, dance and drink coffee rather than visit the library; so why can't we offer them television, films, dancing and coffee *at* the library? And why can we not use the everyday things which interest teenagers to bring them into our buildings? For example, a beautician could give talks at the library on the art of makeup and grooming, with practical demonstrations and (of course) plenty of books available on the subject.

The librarian's attitude to his competitors for teenage leisure time has always been a strange one. Even the old adage 'If you can't beat 'em, join 'em' is inappropriate, for we do not even seem to have been trying to beat 'em!

Surely that should make joining 'em all the easier?

BIBLIOGRAPHY

GENERAL

American Library Association committee on post war planning *The public library plans for the teen age* (American Library Association 1948).

Sheila G Bannister ' Libraries and youth : a survey of progress ' *Library Association record* 66 (1) January 1964 26-8.

Sheila G Bannister ' The public library and the teenage reader ' *Librarian* 49 (8) September 1960 145-9.

Melvyn Barnes ' The forsaken ones ' *Assistant librarian* 57 (10) October 1964 163-70.

H K Gordon Bearman ' Literacy, libraries and youth ' *Book provision for special needs* (Library Association London and Home Counties Branch 1962).

Edwin Castagna ' Library services to youth ' *Library journal* 85 October 15 1960 3611-4.

Douglas Clark ' Library services for children and young people ' *Proceedings of the public libraries conference 1963* (Library Association 1963).

Sara I Fenwick ' Service to young people ' *Library journal* 66 October 15 1941 891-3.

Frank M Gardner ' The public library and the young adult in the United Kingdom ' UNESCO *Bulletin for libraries* 17 (5) September-October 1963 280-4.

Elizabeth Ritts Goebel ' Teenage reading ' *Library journal* 77 (11) June 1 1952 941-3.

Peggy Heeks ' Books for adolescents ' *School librarian* 14 (2) July 1966 133-9.

Frances Henne and others (editors) *Youth, communication and libraries* (American Library Association 1949).

Eric Leyland *The public library and the adolescent* (Grafton 1937).

' The library and the teenager ' (symposium) *Assistant librarian* 56 (6) June 1963 105-23.

Lorna V Paulin ' Young people and the public library ' *School librarian* 15 (1) March 1967 25-31.

Public Library Association committee on standards for work with young adults in public libraries *Young adult services in the public library* (American Library Association 1960).

Jean C Roos ' Young people and public libraries ' *Library trends* 3 (2) October 1954 129-40.

Stanley Rowe ' Libraries and youth ' *Proceedings of the annual conference 1962* (Library Association 1962).

Margaret C Scoggin ' First catch your hare ' ALA *Bulletin* 53 (1) January 1959 55-60.

D H Stock ' Bridging the gap ' *Library Association record* 59 (9) September 1957 298-300.

Helen E Wessells ' The forgotten age group ' ALA *Bulletin* 53 (10) November 1959 827-30 (followed in same issue by replies and comments).

Joseph L Wheeler and Herbert Goldhor *Practical administration of public libraries* (Harper and Row 1962) chapter 20.

Norman W Wood ' There's many a slip twixt . . .' *Assistant librarian* 57 (12) December 1964 200-5.

GENERAL REFERENCES TO WORK IN SOME FOREIGN COUNTRIES

(As most of these articles are in foreign languages the *Library Science abstracts* number has been quoted and the translated titles appear instead of the original titles).

Belgium

L Schevenhels ' Library work with young people in Belgium ' *Openbare bibliotheek* 8 (2) February 1965 22-9 (LSA 66/148).

Canada

Canadian Library Association young people's section *Standards for work with young people in Canadian public libraries* (Canadian Library Association occasional papers (68) December 1966).

Jeanne-M Saint-Pierre ' Work with adolescents ' *Canadian library* 23 (2) September 1966 120-1 (LSA 66/980).

Czechoslovakia

' Work with youth in Brno ' *Ctenár* 16 (12) 1964 414-5 (LSA 15628).

The youth department of the Prague municipal library ' *Ctenár*
15 (12) 1964 389-92 (LSA 14253).

Finland
Annikki Aro ' The departments for children and adolescent
readers in our libraries' *Kirjastolehti* 45 (9) November 1952 205-7
(LSA 3027).

Netherlands
J Daane 'An attempt to define the place of youth library work
within the Dutch library system ' *Openbare bibliotheek* 7 (1)
January 1964 2-12 (LSA 14496).

Sweden
Harald Ahlin ' The libraries and the teenagers ' *Biblioteksbladet*
43 (10) 1958 759-62 (LSA 8880).

Sigurd Mohlenbrock ' The libraries and the young people '
Biblioteksbladet 43 (7) 1958 490-5 (LSA 8354).

Western Germany
Willi Overwien ' Library work with young readers ' *Bücherei und
Bildung* 14 (6) June 1962 278-85 (LSA 12471).

CHAPTER ONE

David P Ausubel *Theory and problems of adolescent development*
(Grune and Stratton 1954).

Robin B Bateman 'Adult books for 13-15 year olds: a report on
the use by secondary grammar school children of a collection of
adult books' *Use of English* 16 (2) Winter 1964 119-28.

Marian E Breckenridge and E Lee Vincent *Child development:
physical and psychologic growth through adolescence* Fourth
edition (W B Saunders 1960).

Luella Cole and Irma Nelson Hall *Psychology of adolescence*
Sixth edition (Holt, Rinehart and Winston 1965).

Marynia F Farnham *The adolescent* (Collier-Macmillan 1962).

Marynia F Farnham ' Who is the young adult?' *Top of the news*
14 October 1957 47-50.

C M Fleming *Adolescence: its social psychology* Second edition
(Routledge and Kegan Paul 1967).

Arnold Gesell and others *Youth: the years from ten to sixteen*
(Hamish Hamilton 1965).

Geneva R Hanna and Mariana K McAllister *Books, young people and reading guidance* (Harper and Row 1960).

Hilde Himmelweit and others *Television and the child: an empirical study of the effects of television on the young* (Oxford University press 1958).

Elizabeth B Hurlock *Adolescent development* Second edition (McGraw-Hill 1955).

A J Jenkinson *What do boys and girls read?* Second edition (Methuen 1946).

Pearl Jephcott *Some young people: a study of adolescent boys and girls* (Allen and Unwin 1954).

Arthur T Jersild *The psychology of adolescence* Second edition (Macmillan 1963).

George W Norvell *The reading interests of young people* (D C Heath 1950).

Neil Postman *Television and the teaching of English* (Appleton-Century-Crofts 1961).

Jacob M Price (editor) *Reading for life: developing the college student's lifetime reading interest* (University of Michigan press 1959).

Timothy Raison (editor) *Youth in New society* (Hart-Davis 1966) (collection of articles which originally appeared in the journal *New society*).

Wilbur Schramm (editor) *The process and effects of mass communication* (University of Illinois press 1954).

W J Scott *Reading, film and radio tastes of high school boys and girls* (Oxford University press 1947).

Mary Stewart ' The leisure activities of grammar school children ' *British journal of educational psychology* 20 (1) February 1950 11-34.

Nicholas Tucker *Understanding the mass media* (Cambridge University press 1966).

W D Wall *The adolescent child* (Methuen 1948).

A R Williams ' The magazine reading of secondary school children ' *British journal of educational psychology* 21 (3) November 1951 186-98.

On intelligence tests
Edgar Anstey *Psychological tests* (Nelson 1966).

A W Heim *The appraisal of intelligence* (Methuen 1954).

Philip E Vernon *Intelligence and attainment tests* (University of London press 1960).

Philip E Vernon *The measurement of abilities* Second edition (University of London press 1956).

On sex education for the adolescent
Maxine Davis *Sex and the adolescent*: *a guide for young people and their parents* (Heinemann 1959).

Bernhardt S Gottlieb *What a boy should know about sex* (Constable 1962).

Bernhardt S Gottlieb *What a girl should know about sex* (Constable 1962).

K H Southall *Lectures to youth clubs on growing up, sex relationships and marriage* (Heinemann 1965).

CHAPTER TWO

Robin B Bateman 'Adult books for 13-15 year olds: a report on the use by secondary grammar school children of a collection of adult books' *Use of English* 16 (2) Winter 1964 119-28.

H K Gordon Bearman 'An enquiry into the use of books and libraries by young people' *Book provision for special needs* (Library Association London and Home Counties Branch 1962).

Joan W Butler 'A study in adolescent reading' *Library Association record* 58 (10) October 1956 387-9.

Central Advisory Council for Education *15 to 18*: *the Crowther report* (HMSO 1959) para 171.

Central Advisory Council for Education *Half our future*: *the Newsom report* (HMSO 1963).

Great Britain Ministry of Education *The education of the adolescent*: *the Hadow report* (HMSO 1927).

Brian Groombridge *Popular culture and personal responsibility*: *a study outline* (National Union of Teachers 1961).

Stuart Hall and Paddy Whannel *The popular arts* (Hutchinson 1964).

Geneva R Hanna and Mariana K McAllister *Books, young people and reading guidance* (Harper and Row 1960).

W G Heath ' Library-centred English : an experiment ' *Educational review* 14 (2) February 1962 98-111.

Hilde Himmelweit and others *Television and the child : an empirical study of the effect of television on the young* (Oxford University press 1958).

David Holbrook *English for maturity* (Cambridge University press 1961).

David L Houldridge ' The reasons why ' *Assistant librarian* 58 (11) November 1965 220-3.

A J Jenkinson *What do boys and girls read?* Second edition (Methuen 1946).

Pearl Jephcott *Some young people : a study of adolescent boys and girls* (Allen and Unwin 1954).

F R Leavis and D Thompson *Culture and environment* (Chatto and Windus 1933).

B Luckham and J M Orr ' Broadcasting and public libraries ' *Library Association record* 69 (1) January 1967 11-13.

Lionel R McColvin *The public library system of Great Britain* (Library Association 1942) page 80.

George Norvell *The reading interests of young people* (D C Heath 1950).

B S Page and P E Tucker ' The Nuffield pilot survey of library use in the University of Leeds ' *Journal of documentation* 15 (1) March 1959 1-11.

Neil Postman *Television and the teaching of English* (Appleton-Century-Crofts 1961).

Jacob M Price (editor) *Reading for life : developing the college student's lifetime reading interest* (University of Michigan press 1959).

Ernest Roe *Teachers, librarians and children* (Crosby Lockwood 1965).

Wilbur Schramm (editor) *The process and effects of mass communication* (University of Illinois press 1954).

W J Scott *Reading, film and radio tastes of high school boys and girls* (Oxford University press 1947).

Mary Stewart ' The leisure activities of grammar school children '
British journal of educational psychology 20 (1) February 1950
11-34.

Denys Thompson (editor) *Discrimination and popular culture*
(Penguin 1964).

Denys Thompson (editor) *Society in focus: an approach to
general studies* (Hutchinson 1961).

Nicholas Tucker *Understanding the mass media* (Cambridge
University press 1966).

A R Williams ' The magazine reading of secondary school
children ' *British journal of educational psychology* 21 (3)
November 1951 186-98.

Raymond Williams *Communications* Revised edition (Chatto and
Windus 1966).

CHAPTER THREE

Mary Askew Backer 'An ounce of prevention ' *Wilson library
bulletin* 35 (4) December 1960 308-11.

Learned T Bulman ' Young adult work in branch libraries '
Library trends 14 (4) April 1966 434-9.

Joan Butler ' Training for tomorrow ' *Library Association record*
65 (4) April 1963 147-50.

Great Britain Ministry of Education *The youth service in England
and Wales: the Albemarle report* (HMSO 1960) para 201.

M F Thwaite ' Training for tomorrow in the youth library
service ' *Library Association record* 59 (2) February 1957 53-6.

CHAPTER FOUR

J G Birkett ' Libraries and the youth service ' *Library assistant* 36
(4) July-August 1943 56-8.

J Macalister Brew ' Library service and youth service ' *Library
Association record* 46 (10) October 1944 179-82.

J Macalister Brew *Youth and youth groups* (Faber 1957).

Great Britain Ministry of Education *Standards of public library
service in England and Wales: the working party report* (HMSO
1962) para 78.

Basil L Q Henriques *Club leadership today* (Oxford University press 1951).

H B Lawson ' The school library, the public library and the school leaver ' *Proceedings of the annual conference 1953* (Library Association 1953).

R O Linden ' Tutor librarianship: a personal view ' *Library Association record* 69 (10) October 1967 351-5.

B S Page and P E Tucker ' The Nuffield pilot survey of library use in the University of Leeds ' *Journal of documentation* 15 (1) March 1959 1-11.

C A Stott *School libraries: a short manual* Second edition (Cambridge University press 1955).

A H Watkins ' The library and the school leaver ' *Librarian* 38 (8) August 1949 193-4.

CHAPTER FIVE

F W S Baguley ' Extension activities in public libraries ' *Library world* 61 (713) November 1959 81-4.

Stephanie Borgwardt *Library display* (Witwatersrand University press 1960).

Robert L Collison *Library assistance to readers* Fifth edition (Crosby Lockwood 1965).

Kate Coplan *Effective library exhibits: how to prepare and promote good displays* (Oceana publications 1958).

Florence S Craig ' Talking about books ' *Library journal* 78 (17) October 1 1953 1601-8.

S Dean 'A great books discussion group ' *Librarian* 42 (5) May 1953 103.

Margaret A Edwards ' Pushing the book ' *Library journal* 91 (22) December 15 1966 6166-8.

Charles A Elliott *Library publicity and service* (Grafton 1951).

S M K Henderson and Helen Kapp *Special exhibitions* (Museums Association 1959).

Cyril O Houle *Libraries in adult and fundamental education* (UNESCO 1951).

Harold Jolliffe *Public library extension activities* (Library Association 1962).

Robert Lee *The library sponsored discussion group* (American Library Association 1957).

Marie D Loiseaux *Publicity primer* Fourth edition (H W Wilson Company 1959).

Lionel R McColvin *Library extension work and publicity* (Grafton 1927).

Patricia Millard *Modern library equipment* (Crosby Lockwood 1966).

Richard B Moses ' Just show the movies—never mind the books! ' ALA *Bulletin* 59 (1) January 1965 58-60.

Ernest A Savage *Manual of book classification and display for public libraries* (Allen and Unwin 1946).

Margaret C Scoggin ' Radio's young book reviewers ' *Library journal* 81 October 15 1956 2416-8.

Carl Thomsen and others *Adult education activities for public libraries* (UNESCO 1950).

Sarah Leslie Wallace *Promotion ideas for public libraries* (American Library Association 1953).

Doris R Watts ' Youth council links school and public library ' *Library journal* 80 January 15 1955 172-3.

Rhyllis Weisjohn ' Bulletin board display ' *Wilson library bulletin* 34 (8) April 1960 569-83.

Index

Page references in italics are to items in the bibliography